EARN IT

Building Your Bank's Brand One
Relationship at a Time

CARL RYDEN, DALLAS WELLS, JIM YOUNG

ABOUT THE AUTHORS

Carl Ryden

Carl Ryden, Co-Founder and Chief Executive Officer of PrecisionLender, has deployed pricing management solutions in hundreds of financial institutions ranging in size from $50 million in assets to over $180 billion in assets. In addition to his work in authoring and developing PrecisionLender's loan pricing system, Carl actively provides strategic consulting to PrecisionLender clients.

His breadth of experience and passion for technology, finance, strategy, and software development enable him to address risk-based pricing from a unique perspective. Carl has an MBA from MIT Sloan School of Management, a Master's Degree in Electrical and Computer Engineering from MIT and a BS in Electrical Engineering from NC State University.

Dallas Wells

Dallas Wells, Executive Vice President Banking Strategies at PrecisionLender, is a banking industry veteran. He has held roles as a commercial lender, CFO, and ALM/Derivatives Consultant, working with banks of all sizes in markets around the country. He has expertise in capital planning, liquidity forecasting, investments, pricing, and interest rate risk. At PrecisionLender, he specializes in helping clients use pricing to improve performance and reduce risk.

Dallas graduated as a Danforth Scholar from Washington University in St. Louis with a BSBA in finance, and is also a graduate of the Southwestern Graduate School of Banking at Southern Methodist University.

Jim Young

Jim Young, Director of Communications at PrecisionLender, is an award-winning writer with experience in a range of positions in media and marketing, from reporter to website editor to content marketer. Throughout his career he has focused on the story – how to find it, how to understand it, and how best to share it with others. At PrecisionLender he manages the many ways in which the company shares its philosophy on banking and the power of relationships

Jim graduated Phi Beta Kappa from Duke University and holds a Master's Degree in journalism from Columbia University.

TABLE OF CONTENTS

INTRODUCTION

Banks today face a tough environment, one that threatens their very existence. The ones that survive, and even thrive, will find their salvation in a surprising place: Pricing.

Have you ever watched *It's A Wonderful Life*? If you're a banker, you really should. If somehow you haven't heard of this movie, then you must not have turned on a television during the month of December. The 1946 film by famed director Frank Capra is a classic—so much so that 70 years later, it remains a staple of the Christmas holiday movie circuit.

It's A Wonderful Life is perhaps the ultimate feel-good movie, about a man who is talked out of suicide by a guardian angel who takes him back through his life, pointing out all the good he's done. The lead character is played by Jimmy Stewart, an actor whose face and voice just scream Main Street America.

Oh, and Stewart's character, George Bailey? He's a banker.

To recap: An actor everyone likes plays a movie character so beloved he has a guardian angel, in a movie with so many good vibes that it's still in heavy rotation 70 years later. And he's a banker.

Scoff if you want, or call it mere coincidence, but know this: Hollywood is all about reflecting current society. So the fact that George Bailey was the heroic head of Bailey Brothers Building and Loan, a man whose loans helped make hopes and dreams come true for the people of Bedford Falls, should tell you how highly regarded bankers once were in America.

George Bailey was a stereotype in its most positive form: the banker as a pillar of his community, a person whom customers trusted and relied upon to help make their lives better.

Nowadays, however, the banker stereotype is not a flattering one. In 2015, while *It's A Wonderful Life* was playing on various cable channels, *The Big Short* was showing in movie theaters. It's about Wall Street investors betting against banks—and winning—during the financial crisis of 2008. A few years earlier, HBO made the movie *Too Big to Fail*, which is about the government assistance banks received during that same time period. It was, to put it mildly, not a flattering piece.

Both movies—and the books they're based on—paint a picture of the banker as the opposite of George Bailey. Bankers are portrayed as greedy, incompetent, and focused much more on some form of a financial shell game than they are on actually helping customers improve their lives.

Perhaps most telling, much of the language is about "the banks," not "bankers." They're portrayed as faceless, monolithic institutions, on the absolute opposite end of the empathy spectrum from George Bailey and his family-owned Bailey Brothers Building and Loan.

Not that bankers have time to worry about what their image is like in Hollywood. They have bigger, real-world problems on their hands. According to the Federal Financial Institutions Examination Council, the number of U.S. commercial banks is down from 14,400 in the first quarter of 1984 to 5,141 in the third quarter of

"The purpose of business is to create and keep a customer." –Peter Drucker

Profit, Drucker argued, is simply the proof that the business is fulfilling its purpose.

2016. Meanwhile, net interest margins have fallen from 4.91% in the first quarter of 1994 to 3.03% in the third quarter of 2016 (Source: FFIEC)[1].

The Sad Story of WaMu

Washington Mutual could serve as poster child for what's gone wrong with banking over the last couple of decades. Opening as a sleepy little thrift on the West Coast in 1889, Washington Mutual—often identified by its nickname, "WaMu"—embodied George Bailey in many ways. They made home loans to individuals and families on a case-by-case basis, growing slowly in both large and small communities. Things suddenly changed, though, when the company "demutualized" in 1983 and converted to a capital stock savings bank. With that conversion came an aggressive new growth strategy.

Following nearly a century of slow and steady growth, WaMu doubled in asset size in the next six years, and then embarked on a spree of more than 30 high-profile acquisitions between 1990 and 2006. As WaMu careened past a quarter trillion dollars in size toward an eventual high of $325 billion, organic growth at rates sufficient to please Wall Street became ever more difficult. Until, that is, the management team found a product type that sold literally as fast as the loans could be processed.

Almost overnight, WaMu became one of the nation's leading producers of Alt-A and Subprime mortgages, including the now infamous option adjustable rate mortgages (ARMs). These magical loans seemed to have unlimited demand, which should have been a blinking red light that something was terribly wrong. In short, WaMu, like much of the rest of the mortgage industry, had badly mispriced their risk in search of outsized growth.

The aftermath was fairly predictable once the marketplace realized what was happening. Keep in mind just how scary September 2008 was in

---

[1]   https://www.ffiec.gov/

the financial markets. That was the month of Bear Stearns being rescued by JP Morgan Chase, Fannie and Freddie entering the protection of conservatorship, and the bankruptcy of Lehman Brothers, just to name a few. Amid that chaos, investors realized that WaMu was in big, big trouble, and funding started to dry up.

On September 15, the holding company received a credit rating downgrade, and over the next 10 days the bank experienced a run on deposits of more than $16 billion. The Office of Thrift Supervision had no choice but to shutter the bank and place it in receivership with the FDIC. They sold the salvageable pieces to JP Morgan Chase for pennies on the dollar, and the once proud and powerful Washington Mutual was erased forever.

Ending with a Whimper

Of course, not all of the decline in banking charters has been driven by spectacular flameouts like Washington Mutual. Thousands of small banks have disappeared with a whimper instead of a bang, throwing up their hands and selling when they realized that they didn't have the capital, the skill set, or the motivation to rebuild their business models for the new information age.

It's sadly reminiscent of what's happened in the world of newspapers. At one point, journalists were heroes, like Woodward and Bernstein, and the papers they wrote for were community institutions. But when the landscape shifted from print to the Internet, newspapers spent years focused on trying to squeeze out the same profit margins rather putting their resources into finding new ways to generate revenue. So far they've succeeded only in slowing down a decline that looks more and more inevitable with each passing year.

How can banks avoid going down a similar path? How can they not only survive but also thrive, and return to their status as Baileyesque pillars of the community?

They can start by listening to Peter Drucker.

Pricing IS the Product

Drucker, the famous business management guru, declared that: "The purpose of business is to create and keep a customer." Profit, Drucker argued, is simply the proof that the business is fulfilling its purpose.

Banks do this when they create value for their customers by forging strong, lasting relationships with them. To do this, banks must rethink pricing: The value they place on it, the strategies they use, and the people and the tools they use to execute those strategies.

In most industries, pricing is just one component of a transaction, where you decide, for instance, how much you are willing to pay for a new phone. In banking, pricing is the product. The dollars loaned are the epitome of a commodity; the speed, flexibility, and responsiveness in structuring and pricing a loan are what allow a bank to differentiate itself and truly build valuable relationships.

Pricing is where the risk management and strategy from the back of the bank meet the sales process and customer interaction in the front of the bank. There is a massive disconnect between these two functions that has led too many banks to choose one or the other. They either go the route of Washington Mutual and forgo sound risk management and discipline in favor of sales targets, or they watch the world pass them by as they try in vain to serve customers using outdated pricing methodologies and sales techniques.

Put simply, pricing is where the rubber meets the road when it comes to relationship-centric banking. To get pricing right, banks have to begin with the lender/customer interaction and work backward from there, always keeping the process focused on strengthening the bond between the banker and the borrower.

That's what we believe at PrecisionLender. It's something we feel so strongly that we were compelled to put our philosophy into words, in this book.

You're welcome to treat this book as a guide, picking and choosing the sections you want to read, but we've also written it to function as a narrative, with each successive section building off the previous one. The full story, from start to finish, is an important one. It applies to every key player at the bank—from the CEO, to the credit analysts, to the people doing the deals.

We'll start by making the case for the importance of pricing to the future of banks. Next, we'll look deeper into the two dimensions of pricing: price setting and price getting. Then we'll talk about where pricing decisions are currently being made in the bank versus where they should be made.

Once we've gone through our philosophical approach to pricing, we'll then turn to the practical side of things and talk about how to turn this thinking into action that leads to stronger relationships and increased revenue. It begins with putting someone in charge of pricing at your bank— your Chief Pricing Officer. Why do you need one? And what qualities should you look for in a CPO?

A CPO is only as good as the people who can "get the prices." So next we'll talk about what makes a great lender. We'll follow that by making the case for bank transparency when it comes to the lending process. Then we'll explain how all of this fits into a bigger picture at your bank, something we call a pricing ecosystem.

After that, we'll get down to the nitty gritty. When you're ready to look into a pricing tool, what should you take into account when choosing a vendor? What mistakes must you avoid? Once you've made those decisions, how can you make sure your lending staff actually takes advantage of the new tools you've given them?

Then, with all your pricing ducks in a row, we'll explain why pricing must be an iterative process, both at the individual lender level and at the institutional level.

Finally, after showing you how your bank can *Earn It* now, we'll give you a glimpse into how you'll *Earn It* in the future.

But enough previewing. Let's get going with getting back to the days when being a banker was truly a wonderful life.

A Few Words about . . . Words

Why "Lenders"?

During the course of writing this book we struggled with what to call the people pricing deals. This is a seemingly simple issue, but as we debated between bankers, lenders, or relationship managers, we actually started unraveling one of the industry's core questions: Who at the bank "owns" the pricing decision and its consequences?

In some banks, the term "lender" has very negative connotations. They feel like the term "lender" oversimplifies the job, making them seem more like order takers who quote the rates to the customer as dictated by the "back of the bank." The term completely ignores the other ways they bring value to the bank beyond just loans. It's an understandable concern.

We had a similar problem with "relationship manager." Again, many of our clients use this term. But so do people in all sorts of industries. It's a bit like the term "account manager" in sales. In some banks the term "relationship manager" is associated with the empty suit, backslapper "salesman" whose job is to play golf with customers. When it comes to the difficult stuff like pricing and negotiating, they will bend to the customer's demands to the detriment of the bank.

We also thought about just using "banker," as it is a term that many of our clients use to refer to themselves. Unfortunately, it doesn't help differentiate the people pricing deals from the people managing those teams, or the people setting prices, and so on. It just wasn't specific enough.

After much back and forth, we decided to go with "lenders."

This book focuses a great deal on building relationships through pricing—the pricing of loans. While that may be only one part of the job, it's clearly a critical component, and it allows us to be specific enough to avoid confusion. So despite having a few warts, "lender" won out.

(Writer nerd note: It's also a lot easier to write sentences that flow when you use "lender" instead of "relationship manager.")

Tool? Platform?

The vast majority of the time in this book we'll refer to the thing lenders use to help price deals as a "pricing tool." But when we refer specifically to the PrecisionLender product—which won't be often—we'll use the term "pricing platform."

"Tool" is a good umbrella term. A pricing platform is a type of pricing tool, one that is capable of working with other tools, one that can grow and change to keep up with the bank's needs, and one that is also capable of learning and improving.

It's a term that's important to our brand, so that's why we use it when talking about our product. But this book isn't sales collateral. We're here to talk about pricing in a more general sense, which is why we use "tool" most often.

(Another writer nerd note: It's also a lot easier to write sentences that flow when you use "tool" instead of "platform.")

CHAPTER 1: WHY IS PRICING SO IMPORTANT?

> "Pricing pressures right now are incredible. The ability to effectively manage pricing will determine the survivors." — President of a regional bank in the Midwest
>
> "It's been my experience, in 30 years of banking, that you win the most what you misprice the worst." — CFO of a regional bank in the Southeast

Wouldn't it be great if you had your own Clarence Odbody, a guardian angel of banking? Someone who could help you shift your attention from all the frustrations and roadblocks in your job and instead get you to focus on the things that matter most, the ones that build your brand and your relationships?

Alas, Odbody is a Hollywood creation. But there are wise men out there, such as Dwight Eisenhower and Stephen Covey, who can offer some valuable guidance.

What's Urgent Versus What's Important

In business and in life it seems we constantly struggle to keep the urgent from crowding out the important.

Each day there is a new fire to put out. When we reach our desks each morning there are dozens, sometimes even hundreds, of new emails at the top of our inbox. Each one is begging for just a few seconds of our attention. Before we know it, the day is gone, then the week, and then the year.

This happens not only at the personal level but at the organizational level as well. There, it's an even harder habit to break. Before you know it, this becomes part of the culture of the organization. Sometimes so much so that the organization completely loses its understanding of what things are, in fact, most important; it only knows what is urgent.

It's an issue that comes up often when we talk with bankers. Banks, especially now in the wake of the Great Recession and the financial crisis, are particularly susceptible to the urgent versus important problem. It is completely understandable: For many banks, over the past few years, addressing the most urgent matters quickly was quite literally a matter of survival. As the economists' saying goes, banks had to make it through the short term to ever make it to the long term.

Put another way, banks were in the first quadrant of the Eisenhower Decision Matrix. The four-quadrant matrix gets its name from the 34th president, who referenced the urgent/important dilemma in a 1954 speech. It's a way of looking at each task in front of you and determining your actions based on those two factors.

URGENCY

	HIGH	LOW
HIGH (IMPORTANCE)	**Q1** **Strategy:** Just do it **Example:** House on fire	**Q2** **Strategy:** Schedule it **Example:** Exercise
LOW (IMPORTANCE)	**Q3** **Strategy:** Delegate/Push Back **Example:** Someone else's urgent deadline	**Q4** **Strategy:** Don't do it **Example:** Refiling last year's important documents

The Eisenhower Matrix

The tasks the banks had to complete to survive during the financial crisis were obviously both important and urgent, a "house on fire situation" for them. Now, with credit portfolios stabilized and improving, and interest rates starting to rise, the importance of some of those tasks has receded, but many banks are struggling to switch out of "urgent" mode. Thus, they're slipping down into the third quadrant.

The goal is to move instead to the second quadrant, where you can look again at the long-term projects that are truly important. Then you've transitioned away from surviving and into thriving.

Putting First Things First

To illustrate this point, Carl often likes to tell the story of the time Stephen Covey, famed author of *The 7 Habits of Highly Effective People*, came to speak to Carl's class when he was a student at MIT's Sloane School of Management.

Covey started out by placing a large glass jar on the table in front of him and filling it with rocks the size of his fist. When no more rocks could fit in the jar, he asked the room, "Is the jar full?"

"Yes," was the audience reply. There was no room left for any more rocks.

Covey then pulled a container of pebbles out from below the table, which he poured into the jar, filling the gaps around the rocks.

"Is it full now?" he asked.

The crowd response this time was mixed. The jar certainly looked full, but the students could sense that Covey was in the midst of making a bigger point. He then reached below the table and produced a container full of sand. He poured that in and it sifted between the pebbles.

"Is the jar full now?"

Now they were certain. "No," was the universal answer.

"Good!" Covey said. Next he poured water into the jar, filling it up to the top.

"So what was the point of this? What is the lesson to be learned here?" he asked. This was a room full of "Type A" overachievers at a top MBA program. The answer was obvious to all of them: If you are creative, diligent, and persistent, you can always find time to do one more thing. You can always add one more thing to your to-do list or squeeze one more project into the plan for the next year. Even when your life seems full, you can always add more if you try hard enough.

Covey smiled and then pulled a neat bit of mental jiu jitsu on the room.

"No, the lesson here is that if I hadn't put the big rocks in first, I would never have been able to get them into the jar."

Covey went on, "In your business and in your life, you have to put forth effort to identify the 'big rocks' and then make sure that you put those in the jar first, or they will never make it in there."

Every day banks spend countless dollars and hours on projects such as compliance training, IT infrastructure projects, core data cleanups, mobile apps, and network security projects. All of them have a feeling of urgency, but are they truly central to the mission of the bank? Are they helping to build stronger relationships with the customer and to increase revenue?

If not, then they're the pebbles and sand in Covey's demonstration.

Getting pricing right? That's a big rock. The biggest, actually.

"A strategy based on cutting prices to increase volumes and, as a result, to raise profits is generally doomed to failure in almost every market and industry."

This isn't breaking news; it's the way of the business world.

The Impact of Pricing

Bankers know this. They know that pricing is one of the primary determinants of performance. Still, they often underestimate the degree to which pricing impacts their bank. Back in 2003, the consulting firm McKinsey & Co. published an influential article called "The Power of Pricing."[2] It reached some pretty eye-opening conclusions.

---

[2] "The power of pricing", February 2003, McKinsey Quarterly, www.mckinsey.com. Copyright (c) 2003 McKinsey & Company. All rights reserved. Reprinted by permission.

Using the average income statement of an S&P 1500 company as its standard, McKinsey found that a "price rise of 1%, if volumes remained stable, would generate an 8% increase in operating profits."

McKinsey compared that to cost-cutting and found that the impact of a 1% price rise was "nearly 50% greater than that of a 1% fall in variable costs such as materials and direct labor."

The numbers were even more dramatic when comparing a price increase to a corresponding 1% increase in volume. Price's impact on profits was nearly three times that of volume.

And as McKinsey put it, "The sword of pricing cuts both ways." A 1% decrease in average prices leads to an 8% decrease in profits if the other factors remain stable. McKinsey considered a theoretical 5% price cut for one of those sample S&P companies and found that the company would have to increase sales volume by 18.7% just to bring things back to even in that scenario.

If you're a bank tempted to drop rates so you can pry a few deals away from the competitor down the street, or perhaps just to keep up with the new bank in town that's turning heads, McKinsey offered this sober warning: "A strategy based on cutting prices to increase volumes and, as a result, to raise profits is generally doomed to failure in almost every market and industry."

The McKinsey piece is a powerful article that's still frequently cited in business, but it's worth noting that it came out 12 years ago. This isn't breaking news; it's the way of the business world. It's time for banks to adjust to this reality.

In fact, you could argue that pricing is even more vital to the future of banks than to other businesses.

Before we go further, let's note that when we discuss pricing in this book, we're talking about commercial loan pricing. While there are many other areas in which banks price—checking, mobile banking, CDs, etc.—they have become essentially commoditized. Commercial lending is where the most value remains, where improvements in pricing can have the biggest effect.

Make a splash with the big rock of pricing and here are some of the places touched by the ripples:

- How you approach pricing and the management of pricing has a huge impact on the nature of the conversations your lenders can have with borrowers. If your pricing is flawed, you wind up with the "used car salesman" scenario, in which a lender negotiates a deal once with the borrower, then negotiates it again with the rest of the bank, and then re-trades it with the borrower. That's damaging not only to that particular opportunity but to the overall relationship.

- Pricing has a huge impact on which relationships you win, which ones you lose, and how much you get paid in each deal.

- The pricing decisions you make today will determine the portfolio you're going to have to live to with in the future, both in terms of interest rate risk and credit risk.

- Along those lines, pricing is one of the main ways you communicate to the marketplace where you would like to deploy your capital and what sort of assets you'd like to bring in. Sending out the wrong message can have disastrous consequences. As a bank executive once told us: "It's been my experience, in 30 years of banking, that you win the most what you misprice the worst."

Given the importance of pricing to banks, it should come as no surprise then that any small improvement on that front can have an enormous impact.

Pricing Is a Game of Inches

Al Pacino has a great speech in the movie *Any Given Sunday*. In the film, Pacino plays the role of a professional football coach. Before the team's big game, he gives an inspiring pregame pep talk about "the inches."

You can check out the full version (with some of Pacino's more "colorful" language removed) at the end of this chapter. But for now, this excerpt will work just fine.

> You find out that life is just a game of inches. So is football. Because in either game life or football, the margin for error is so small. I mean one half-step too late or too early and you don't quite make it. One half-second too slow or too fast, and you don't quite catch it. The inches we need are everywhere around us. They are in every break of the game, every minute, every second.

Now, Pacino is trying to rile up a bunch of big, burly football players, but you also could drop him in a banker's conference and have him give the same speech (although perhaps without the profanity). For banks, the inches they need are absolutely everywhere around them. They can be found in pricing, on both the lender and the institutional level.

The competitive landscape in banking right now is such that deals are often won or lost on the smallest differences. You know those situations when you're pricing a deal, you feel like you've almost closed it, and then at the last second you find out you lost. You missed out because of this tiny, seemingly insignificant thing—maybe something you didn't even really care about. You would have gladly included it in your offer if you'd known it was going to be the deciding factor. Maybe it was a few basis points here, a pre-penalty payment there, or a personal guarantee that the borrower really didn't want to add.

The key here is that "the inches" bankers need are not necessarily found by increasing the rates on the loans. Commercial loans have hundreds of variables. Each one of them impacts the risk-adjusted profit to the bank and the appeal to the borrower. Incremental changes to just a few of these variables might make the difference in winning that deal or losing it.

That's the lender level. On the institutional level, each of those deals your bank wins (or loses) becomes one of the inches. Every single loan you price goes into the creation of the bank's balance sheet. Price well loan by loan, inch by inch, and you end up with a stable, profitable bank. Make mistakes like mispricing risk relative to the rest of the market, and each of those bad loans piles up, inch by inch, until you're Washington Mutual.

Let's go back to the McKinsey pricing article for a moment and borrow that 1% improvement figure. Plug that in for an anonymous bank that has a commercial loan portfolio of around $5 billion and yields at 4%. A 1% improvement for this bank translates to about 4 basis points. On $5 billion, those additional 4 basis points (i.e., a 0.04% increase in yield) produce $2 million a year, just on that commercial loan portfolio. And the beauty is that a commercial loan book usually turns over really fast, so you can get to those results faster than you can in other industries. For the bank in this example, it would actually take a little less than 20 months to hit that number.

And that's just using the assumption that we're improving the pricing on the loans we win. What if, on top of that incremental improvement, we found ways to win more of the deals we'd previously been losing by those inches? What if we win just one out of 20 of those deals that we're missing today? How does that change the picture? What about one in 10? Find ways to pick up some of those, and now the 4 basis points start to look like chump change.

Treating the Symptoms, Not the Disease

Maybe you're not convinced that pricing is the way to find those inches. What if you went looking for them elsewhere? What if you left pricing alone and simply looked to keep your margins high by cutting costs?

The McKinsey article addressed this, with a bit of a "been there, done that" attitude, way back in 2003, noting that, "at many companies, little cost-cutting juice can be easily extracted from operations." Even if, 14 years later, there is still a little bit of blood remaining to be squeezed from the stone, at best cost-cutting can be only part of the solution. Banks that are looking at cost-cutting as THE solution are essentially treating the symptoms, not the disease.

Again, newspapers have already blazed this grim trail. When the Internet changed the advertising game forever, newspapers prioritized cost-cutting over searching for new revenue streams to replace those that were drying up. Shrinking staffs also lessened the quality of the product, putting a dent in newspapers' brand image as the most trusted news sources in their communities. Newspapers got short-term profit-margin results (the "symptoms") but never found a way to solve their long-term revenue problem (the disease).

Actually, maybe newspapers are too bleak an example to use. There's an argument to be made that there never was a cure to the disease for them, that newspapers are simply an outdated technology that has to go the way of horse-drawn buggies and eight-track tapes. That's not the case with banking. Every day we work with banks that are fixing their ailing bottom lines by focusing on effective pricing.

What Effective Pricing Looks Like

The data in this section comes from two groups of banks. The first is our clients, who we know use the pricing methodology outlined in this book. The second is all other banks, some of which may use the methodology but many of which do not.

- PrecisionLender's publicly traded clients have achieved 93% market capitalization growth over the five-year period of June 2010 to June 2015 compared to the KBW NASDAQ Bank Index's 60% growth.

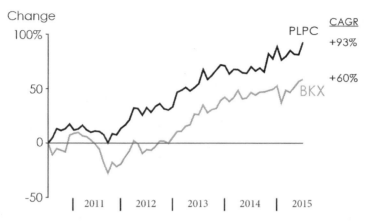

PLPC: a market camp weighted composite index of all PrecisionLender publicly traded clients
BKX: the KBW NASDAQ Bank Index

- All clients with more than $1 billion in assets improved their NIM by 18.9 basis points more than their peers over the two-year period from June 2013 to June 2015 after implementing PrecisionLender.

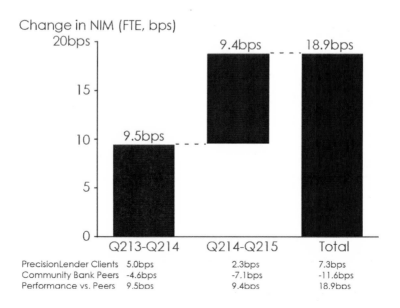

	Q213-Q214	Q214-Q215	Total
PrecisionLender Clients	5.0bps	2.3bps	7.3bps
Community Bank Peers	-4.6bps	-7.1bps	-11.6bps
Performance vs. Peers	9.5bps	9.4bps	18.9bps

- All clients with more than $1 billion in assets outpaced their peers by 5.7% in annual loan growth over the two-year period from June 2013 to June 2015 after implementing PrecisionLender.

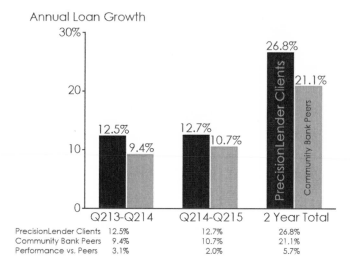

Annual Loan Growth

	PrecisionLender Clients	Community Bank Peers	Performance vs. Peers
Q213-Q214	12.5%	9.4%	3.1%
Q214-Q215	12.7%	10.7%	2.0%
2 Year Total	26.8%	21.1%	5.7%

All PrecisionLender clients over $1B in assets, who were clients for the full period covered, versus community banks over $1B and less than $50B in assets. Source: SNL Financial

We'll dive more deeply into an individual bank's pricing success in Chapter 5, when we make the case for a Chief Pricing Officer. But there are a few more steps we need to take before we get there. We've argued for why we think pricing is important. Now it's time to talk about what goes into the actual act of pricing and why relationships are central to that effort.

"The Inches" Speech from Any Given Sunday[3]

I don't know what to say really.

Three minutes to the biggest battle of our professional lives

All comes down to today.

Either we heal as a team, or we're going to crumble.

---

[3]   Any Given Sunday, Directed by Oliver Stone. Los Angeles, CA: Warner Bros. Studio, 1999.

Inch by inch, play by play, till we're finished.

We are in hell right now, gentlemen, believe me,

And we can stay here and get the s— kicked out of us

Or we can fight our way back into the light.

We can climb out of hell, one inch at a time.

Now I can't do it for you, I'm too old.

I look around and I see these young faces and I think . . .

I mean, I made every wrong choice a middle-aged man could make.

I, uh, I pissed away all my money, believe it or not.

I chased off anyone who has ever loved me.

And lately I can't even stand the face I see in the mirror.

You know when you get old in life things get taken from you.

That's . . . that's part of life.

But you only learn that when you start losing stuff.

You find out that life is just a game of inches. So is football.

Because in either game, life or football, the margin for error is so small.

I mean, one half-step too late or too early and you don't quite make it.

One half-second too slow or too fast and you don't quite catch it.

The inches we need are everywhere around us.

They are in every break of the game, every minute, every second.

On this team, we fight for that inch.

On this team, we tear ourselves, and everyone around us, to pieces for that inch.

We CLAW with our finger nails for that inch.

Because we know when we add up all those inches

That's going to make the f—— difference

Between WINNING and LOSING

Between LIVING and DYING.

I'll tell you this:

In any fight it is the guy who is willing to die who is going to win that inch.

And I know if I am going to have any life anymore

It is because I am still willing to fight and die for that inch

Because that is what LIVING is, the six inches in front of your face.

Now I can't make you do it.

You gotta look at the guy next to you.

Look into his eyes.

Now, I think you are going to see a guy who will go that inch with you.

You are going to see a guy who will sacrifice himself for this team

Because he knows when it comes down to it,

You are gonna do the same thing for him.

That's a team, gentlemen.

And either we heal now, as a team,

Or we will die as individuals.

That's football guys.

That's all it is.

Now, whattaya gonna do?

CHAPTER 2: PRICE SETTING

"You can't out-math the competition." — Carl Ryden

F ollowing the financial crisis of 2008–2009 and the subsequent deep recession, a multi-billion dollar bank in the Midwest was at an important crossroads. The bank had in essence been born during the crisis, as a large investor arranged several shotgun weddings of smaller banks that were either failing or were run by management teams that didn't feel equipped to deal with the changes facing the industry.

The resulting bank in some ways resembled Frankenstein's monster, as the various pieces didn't seem to fit together exactly right. In fact, for this story we'll call it Frankenstein Bank. There was a core piece that was a traditional community bank, with high concentrations in commercial real estate, but there were also smaller offices spread all over the country, with lending focuses in areas such as energy, entertainment, and gaming. They all had different management teams, and each had its own culture that dictated everything from credit standards to pricing practices. The new leadership at Frankenstein Bank had their work cut out for them, to say the least.

After putting the basic underwriting process in place, the bank's management team shifted its attention to pricing. Like a lot of banks, they turned to trusty old Microsoft Excel and went about expanding on a risk-adjusted return on capital model from one of the precursor banks to price loans.

The finance folks did their homework and covered all the bases. They built a bank-specific funding curve with a built-in liquidity premium. They debated which interpolation method was best. They did extensive studies of overhead costs, and they built credit migration assumptions. They even started a massive project that would enable them to use stochastic modeling to allocate economic capital for individual loans based on their specific credit profile.

However, despite the thousands of dollars and hundreds of hours spent on pricing over a three-year period, Frankenstein Bank's results were lagging far behind those of its peers. Specifically, despite growing the loan portfolio at an impressive clip and improving the loan/deposit ratio, the bank's net interest margins were shrinking. And not just by a little. As the chart below shows, net interest margins declined by more than 100 basis points. For a bank that size, that's about $70 million per year worth of margin.

Frankenstein Bank NIM

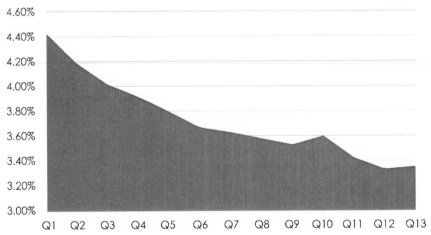

So, why didn't these efforts translate to results? After all, Frankenstein Bank clearly realized the importance of pricing and was willing to spend the time and money necessary to improve in this area. Why were the prices they had spent immense effort to calculate so precisely not the ones that were actually landing on their books? And why weren't they building valuable relationships with their customers that would translate to premium pricing?

The bank was coming to realize what many before had found: You can't simply "out- math" the competition. No matter how good you are at Price Setting, to price effectively you have to be equally good at Price Getting.

"Don't let perfect be the enemy of good."

Pricing is a forward-looking, prospective exercise, and as such, it can get messy.

The Two Dimensions of Pricing

Pricing is hard. This is one of those universal truths that applies to every business, and it is certainly true in banking. The difficulty lies in the fact that pricing is inherently cross- functional. You need inputs from lots of different sources, both internal and external, and you have to please numerous stakeholders that all have different perspectives and end goals. And in banking there is the added complexity that you are pricing financial instruments, which adds degrees of both math and risk that aren't found in most industries.

Every bank in the world struggles with pricing, and just when they start to get comfortable with it, there is a fundamental shift in either their own bank or in the market at large, and they have to start over.

But why is this? Why is pricing, which is the essence of the banking business, such a struggle for so many?

To answer that big question, let's start with the research of Stephan Liozu, author of *The Pricing Journey*[4]. Liozu describes two dimensions of pricing capability, Price Setting and Price Getting, and shows that to excel at pricing, companies must master both dimensions.

We'll tackle Price Setting in this chapter and then turn our attention to Price Getting in Chapter 3. Brace yourself, because right now we're going to go into full bank-nerd mode.

Why Bankers Prefer Price Setting

Price Setting is what gets all of the attention in the banking business. Why? Because it's math. Most bankers pride themselves on analytics and on being able to quantify a deal in a neat and tidy box.

---

[4] Liozu, Stephan. The pricing journey: the organizational transformation toward pricing excellence. Stanford, CA: Stanford Business , an imprint of Stanford U Press, 2015. Print.

Even though Price Setting is the dimension that gets the most attention, that doesn't mean all banks are good at it. There's plenty of evidence to the contrary in the marketplace. Still, given the comfort level with the concepts and the fact that progress should be quantifiable, bankers almost universally choose fixing this dimension as the way to correct their pricing woes. This approach makes sense, as Price Setting is the foundation for everything else.

Although the range of Price Setting skill in banks is very wide, there are a few common stumbling blocks. Before we jump into these, there is a conceptual framework we need to establish first.

As much as it pains bankers, when it comes to Price Setting, they need to live by the old saying, "Don't let perfect be the enemy of good." Pricing is a forward-looking, prospective exercise, and, as such, it can get messy.

There is no such thing as 100% accuracy, and bankers (especially the finance types) get uncomfortable with the uncertainty. They know the importance of pricing, so there is an urge to get the assumptions just right. And many, like Frankenstein Bank, will spend years trying to get everything perfected. In the meantime, they are pricing millions of dollars in loans with an old tool they know is flawed.

Instead, banks should use a "continuous deployment" mentality, whereby they can roll out the improved methodology—after all, it is better than what you have!—and slowly refine it over time. All of this should happen with the understanding that perfection is not the goal. There will come a point when gaining the extra degree of accuracy is not worth the time, resources, or interference with end users needed to achieve it.

Finding the Right Funding Costs

With that said, there are a few common Price Setting issues we see banks struggling with on a regular basis. First is the fundamental question of what to use for funding costs. There are still a number of banks that insist they should be pricing off their internal cost of funds. Their thinking:

"Don't we want to know the true profitability of this loan we are about to book?"

From an accounting perspective, yes, you will want to measure true profits. However, balancing back to the GAAP financial statements is not the goal of pricing, nor is it making the ideal accounting decision. The goal is to make the best economic decision. If you have ever spent time studying the inner workings of banks' financial statements, you know that accounting and economic decisions are often at odds with each other. You already spend plenty of money on balancing the debits and credits and reporting on how much money you made yesterday. This is about making optimal decisions to make more money tomorrow, and the inputs should be different.

At first blush, pricing off an internal funding cost seems very logical. This method, however, almost always results in underpricing loans in a rising rate environment and overpricing loans in a declining rate environment. This occurs because an internal funding cost is a historical number and includes deposits with varying maturities. As a result, an internal funding cost moves much more slowly than an incremental funding cost and thus will lag the true market rates where assets are being booked.

In addition to having a funding cost that reflects a historic cost versus a current funding cost, there is also the question of what premium should be charged for pricing out on the funding curve. In other words, how much more should you charge a borrower to lock in a rate for five years compared to three years? How much does your pricing change for a floating rate loan?

The better answer is to use a market-based curve that represents a realistic marginal funding source for you. Although you can't fund your bank exclusively with FHLB advances, you can buy money at exactly the rate posted. These rates change daily and move with general market rates. Most community banks use FHLB, and then, as banks get larger, they tend to use the LIBOR swap curve as the basis for funding costs.

You can certainly adjust the curve as needed to reflect things such as your liquidity premium or your own exposure to rate movements, but the important takeaway is that the funding curve moves with market rates and is not skewed by your own accounting of historical decisions.

What to Do with Overhead Costs

The next big stumbling block is overhead costs. The indecision here usually stems from having to choose between using fully absorbed overhead for the loan department versus just using the incremental cost to originate and service an individual loan.

A simple question should help here. Do your borrowers care if you have high overhead? Are they willing to pay more just because you have an expensive branch network, or spend more than your peers on health insurance? Of course not! You don't want to avoid making a loan because you have high overhead; if anything, you want to make more loans to help carry that burden.

Instead, you should be measuring the marginal cost to get the loan on the books. The goal is to find the optimal place to invest available funds, not to tie back to accounting results.

Measuring Credit Risk and Allocating Capital

The final stumbling block is one that is admittedly not simple to solve. How do you measure credit risk and allocate capital?

The perception of capital in the banking industry has changed dramatically over the last several years. Banks were almost always viewed (at least internally) as having excess capital. While perhaps this was true, the biggest mistake that resulted from this belief was a drive for growth without a corresponding pricing differentiation based on quality.

Regardless of the cause, the important thing is to arm lenders to compete aggressively for the best-quality loans, and to be well compensated for all other borrowers. Due to the new Basel standards, capital is now the bottleneck for growth, and as a precious resource it needs to be allocated in the most efficient and profitable way possible. More risk in a deal should translate to more capital, and therefore more revenue to justify making that loan.

Yet for most banks, there is little difference in how they price a strong credit and a weak credit. If all borrowers are priced close to average, then the bank is overcharging the best borrowers and undercharging the worst. Is this really the strategy to pursue, aggressively chasing the borrowers who are the least desirable?

The differentiation of pricing based on quality is in flux in the industry, as there is a slow transformation occurring from a single-factor approach to a multi-factor approach. In the single-factor approach, the loan loss reserve and credit capital are based on the risk rating for the loan. The risk rating for the loan includes all the underwriting criteria, such as exposure at default, risk of default, collateral, and guarantors. In other words, after considering each of these items, the lender comes up with one number that represents the credit risk of the loan.

The multi-factor approach seeks to be more precise about the actual risk of the loan, the probability of the default, and the anticipated loss in the event of default. As such, the risk of the borrower, the type and value of collateral, and the type and amount of the guarantees are all considered separately instead of being combined into one risk factor.

The risk of the borrower tells the probability of default. From there, you would use the facility details (exposure at default, collateral, and guarantees) to determine a loss given default.

The big takeaway, though, is that you do not need to be 100% accurate. In fact, that is impossible when pricing a prospective transaction in which you have to make so many guesses about what will happen in the future.

The goal is to be directionally correct, giving your lenders the ability to price more aggressively to win the very best deals and making sure you are adequately compensated for the risk and uncertainty in all of the other deals. Point yourself in the right direction with an approach and a tool that are better than what you have, and then refine it over time.

As you can see from the few issues we covered here, the Price Setting isn't easy. The concepts might make sense, but there will still be internal disagreements based on the differing perspectives. The finance team has different incentives than the credit team, and both will often be at odds with the loan team. Once the concepts are settled, the execution can be tricky. We haven't even touched on some of the heavier math involved in deciding between using regulatory capital versus economic capital, or how to treat caps and floors, or what to do with prepayment penalties.

The good news is that there are industry standards and many resources available to fix Price Setting, so you should be able to continue making incremental progress forward.

The bad news? Without mastering the second dimension, Price Getting, all of that Price Setting work is for naught.

CHAPTER 3: PRICE GETTING

> Without effective pricing, your bank will be the one everyone comes to last so they can shave their rate by another eighth of a point.

P rice Getting covers people and process issues, but it essentially boils down to one question: How good are you at actually booking the price after you set it?

Like Frankenstein Bank in Chapter 2, many banks are discovering they can't just "out- math" the competition. It does no good to be really great at setting prices if you end up discounting deals to get them on the books or losing deals because you couldn't find a creative way to make them meet your targets. So, what is Price Getting and how do banks get better at it in a way that builds relationships and positively affects the bank's brand? That is the focus of the rest of this book, but in this chapter we will introduce some of the big concepts.

Price Getting covers all the people and process issues involved in actually booking the price that is set. We describe these two functions with the terms "back of the bank" and "front of the bank." The back of the bank focuses on Price Setting and typically includes all of the finance, credit, and risk management inputs that go into calculating an acceptable risk-based price. The front of the bank is the sales and production staff who get the customers to agree to those prices. The act of balancing Price Setting with Price Getting can be difficult, but it is an absolutely vital task for banks.

As we've noted, pricing is an inherently cross-functional task, and bridging the gap between Price Setting and Price Getting (i.e., the back of the bank and the front of the bank) is very difficult. We've pointed out that there are a lot of resources to fix Price Setting, as it is the foundation upon which we build everything else. But once the math is in place, how important is the Price Getting part?

> *"Effective pricing is at least 90% effective selling."*

We put it pretty bluntly when talking to our clients, telling them that "effective pricing is at least 90% effective selling." That effective selling component is far reaching, but here are the biggest components to get you started.

Pricing Alignment

The first step to successful Price Getting is the proper alignment of pricing within the bank's overall strategy. This may seem like an obvious first step, but we often see a huge disconnect between marketing and reality. In other words, banks try to price like the Ritz but their customer base and service levels are more like Motel 6. Or vice versa, as a miss either way is a problem.

For further illustration, let's start with a pretty common statement from bankers. "I'm not sure you understand. Our market is REALLY competitive, and there is just no way we can get those kinds of rates here."

We hear some version of that statement every time we talk to a new bank. And we don't mean most of the time. *Every* time we talk to a bank, someone tells us that the pricing philosophy we are describing might work in a lot of places, but it just won't work in a market that's as competitive as theirs is.

Now, we should clarify that we believe those statements. We can see in the data just how brutal the competition is for the best loans, and we can also see that just about every market has "that bank" that is putting painfully aggressive pricing in front of your customers and prospects.

Our assertion, though, is that while your current approach might make it impossible to "get those kinds of rates" on the best deals, there is another approach that will get you there. However, the answer is not to simply tell your lenders to hold the line on a particular rate, or to be better at the math. Instead, you have to first do a little homework so you can better arm your lenders to approach the right kind of borrowers with the right kind of deal.

Don't Just "Sell More Stuff"

The best place to start is with a solid game plan. We find an awful lot of banks that are still haphazard in their approach to the market, with the only strategy being to "sell more stuff to more customers." Heck, if we're honest, we have struggled with this exact problem ourselves. The issue is covered in a *Harvard Business Review* article called "Don't Turn Your Sales Team Loose Without a Strategy," written by Frank Cespedes and Steve Thompson[5]. This passage in particular is applicable to banks:

> "The problem is few firms clarify their deal-selection criteria. Either directly in meetings or implicitly in their compensation plans, they basically tell their sales forces to 'Go forth and multiply!' And that is exactly what happens.
>
> As a consequence, salespeople tend to sell to anyone they can, often at discounted prices to make a volume quota target. There are also opportunity costs: as money, time, and people are allocated to customer A, they are not available to customers B, C, and so on.

---

[5]   Cespedes, Frank V., and Steve Thompson. "Don't Turn Your Sales Team Loose Without a Strategy." Harvard Business Review. N.p., 15 Dec. 2015. Web. 17 Feb. 2017. <https://hbr.org/2015/12/dont-turn-your-sales-team-loose-without-a-strategy>.

This is ineffective deal management, and it eventually leads to loss of positioning with customers, and, over time, the nurturing of 'commodity competencies.' In other words, the sales force gets better and better at striking deals that more customers value less and less."

Wishful Lending

Does any of that sound familiar? How many banks give their lenders a portfolio growth number and then send them on their way? Especially for community banks, trying to be all things to all people is a dangerous strategy. The big guys are playing the same game, and they are exceptionally good at it.

The real problem is what the authors describe as the "nurturing of commodity competencies." We all know what this looks like in the world of commercial lending. It means that most banks in a market offer similar terms, and the only differentiator is rate. The question you have to ask is, what do you want your brand to be? Do you want to be the bank that everyone comes to last so they can shave the rate by another eighth of a point? Or do you want to be the bank that everyone comes to first because they know you will be creative and fair in finding a deal that best fits their needs?

Let's say a borrower tells you they are buying a commercial property, and you look up your current price for a standard deal. In some markets this is a 5-year balloon on a 25-year amortization schedule, and in others it might be a fully amortizing 15-year deal, but the point is that most banks are afraid to offer something markedly different from what the borrower is seeing from competitors. So, you put your deal on the table and hope that your lender is tight enough with the borrower that you can win without having the lowest bid. Did you take them to play golf enough times?

But, as Cespedes and Thompson say, "Hope is not a strategy."

Identify the Good Deals

You need to be able to offer real value to that borrower. For example, consider Bill Ragle, a lender at Comerica Bank. His team specializes in lending to medical groups, and they don't have to win deals with low rates. Instead, they build relationships by making life easier for their borrowers and providing advice that has real value because they know the industry inside and out. You don't get that by being all things to all people.

Start by understanding what the "good deals" are for your bank. Which ones are profitable, and which ones are you really good at? Then, spend your time and effort figuring out a way to get more of those, and spend less time chasing everything else. If you do those deals better than anyone else in your market, and you can be creative in finding ways to make them work for your borrowers, you'll find yourself in far fewer bidding wars.

Communicating the Price

Communicating is really about the tools used to translate pricing from the back of the bank to the front. These range from the old-fashioned printed rate sheet to full-blown enterprise-level pricing platforms like PrecisionLender.

Whatever tool you use, your lenders need more than just the "sticker price" for each product. They also need to know where the line in the sand is for pricing exceptions and customized structures. Banks complain about their products being commoditized, but they often become the primary instigators of that mentality by limiting the ability of their lenders to price anything that isn't predefined on the rate sheet. To be truly effective, you need to communicate clear targets and boundaries to your lenders, as well as the relative value of each deal component. If the only lever they can move is the rate, expect to see a lot of discounts.

Negotiation Framework

Related to that concept is the creation of a basic framework for negotiating. The top-performing banks have clear boundaries set for negotiations between lenders and borrowers, and the lenders have authority to agree to pricing within those ranges. In addition, they also have clarity and efficiency built into the approval process for any deals outside the boundaries.

The other banks? That's where we still see a lot of the "let me check with my manager" approach to negotiations that people detest so much from their car-buying experiences, and way too many response times measured in weeks instead of minutes. When the customer experience suffers to this degree, the bank can't expect to get premium pricing.

Lender Training

The industry is facing an acute shortage of experienced and productive commercial lenders. This shortage is tied directly to the majority of banks killing off their formal training programs, leaving no pipeline of home-grown lending talent. Has your bank trained lenders on how to effectively sell your value proposition? Do your lenders know how to negotiate with their borrowers? A few banks have gone the extra mile with this and they are in the process of eating everyone else's lunch.

Lender Incentives and Accountability

This concept is straightforward, although the execution of it can admittedly get overly complex in a hurry. The basic idea is that while bankers will complain to lenders about the compressing spreads on their deals, lenders know what REALLY matters when the year-end review comes around. No matter how many metrics or reports are shown to them, it's all about portfolio growth. Is your personal portfolio up 25%? Then you are golden, and there are raises and promotions headed your way.

We talk a good game about loan profitability, but very few banks actually measure and reward their lenders based on profitability. Give them some real incentive to balance profitability and growth just like the bank as a whole must do, and you will be amazed at how well your lenders respond.

You can see why Price Setting receives more attention than Price Getting. The Getting is really hard and requires some organizational change that won't happen overnight. The good news though, is that it is also an incredibly powerful lever for improving performance. You don't have to get it perfect right out of the gate, and you don't have to tackle it all at once; even incremental changes will quickly translate to better results. Just remember that you have to balance both dimensions, and you have to bridge the gap between the front and back of your bank. Do that well, and you are on your way to being a high-performing bank with happy lenders AND happy borrowers.

What Kind of Bank Are You?

Now that we have outlined the two dimensions of pricing, what does success or failure look like along those dimensions? In other words, what are the consequences of ignoring one dimension?

While determining the exact cause of the failures in pricing can be difficult, the outcomes are pretty straightforward. Are you wondering which aspect of your pricing approach needs work? An honest appraisal of where you fall on the diagram below should point you in the right direction.

The Pushovers   The Champs

The Reckless Gunslingers   The Stubborn Old Mules

PRICE SETTING

PRICE GETTING

The Reckless Gunslingers

These banks are a dwindling breed (since they keep failing), but we still run across more than you might expect. They are the banks that are terrible at setting the right price for their credit and interest rate risks and are willing to discount from there when necessary. These banks are dangerous, not just to themselves, but to everyone else in their market. If you have any borrowers that you are worried about, this is exactly where you should point them.

The Stubborn Old Mules

These banks struggle with Price Setting but stick to their guns once they come to a decision. The problem is that the prices they are defending don't always make sense. Sometimes they are stubbornly staying with above-market rates in search of margin and are sacrificing top-line growth to get it (look for the giant bond portfolios).

Other times they have set prices for certain structures too low and stick to them even when the outsized production should tell them they got it wrong (look for the concentrations in risky loan types or long-term fixed rates).

These banks have the shortest path to improvement, but in our experience they are also the least likely to actually take it. After all, they already have it figured out, thank you very much.

The Pushovers

This quadrant represents most of the larger banks. They have sophisticated tools and entire teams dedicated to calculating the right price . . . usually out to four decimal places. The trouble is that the lenders trying to book deals at those rates find it impossible because they don't have access to those same tools, they haven't been properly trained, or they know they can simply ignore the nerds with the calculators.

These banks are the hardest to fix, as massive organizational change is far more daunting than simply improving the math. The good news (or bad, if they are a competitor) is that a growing number are willing to try, as the results are impossible to ignore.

The Champs

The rarest of all are the banks in the top right corner that are good at both Price Setting and Price Getting. You can spot these banks from a distance because they are the ones that are growing like crazy while still generating top decile earnings.

When asked about performance, their leaders never talk about pricing methodology. Instead they talk about relationships and their strong teams. What they are really saying is that they've mastered the Price Getting component that eludes most of their peers.

So, which category best describes your bank? The right fix depends on a proper diagnosis, and, in most cases, better math alone won't fix your performance.

Our friends at Frankenstein Bank came to exactly that conclusion. They had spent plenty of time and money on the Price Setting, but had completely ignored the Price Getting dimension. The solution for them has been to invest in the tools, processes, and people to pay more attention to one aspect of their business that had been largely ignored: that pesky little detail called the customers.

CHAPTER 4: MOVING THE PRICING PROCESS FORWARD

> Are your tools empowering your lenders? Or second-guessing them?

As you've probably noticed by now, we like to use stories to help make our points when discussing our pricing philosophy. So we'll start this chapter with another one, a hypothetical step-by-step account of a borrower trying to make his way through the traditional loan process. Along the way, we'll keep track of the time spent for each step, as well as the total process time.

The Traditional (Slow) Borrowing Process

Step 1. The borrower comes to the bank to discuss a loan request. If they are experienced borrowers they will bring most of the financial documents needed. (If not, the bank will request financials before discussing any terms, adding a week to the process right off the bat.) At this meeting, the bank will usually quote something from the rate sheet or standard starting structure. If the borrower wants anything different, the lender replies, "Let me check with my boss."

Step 2. The lender consults with his boss, who says, "If the underwriting is good and the deal hurdles (i.e., it has a sufficient ROE when plugged into the pricing model), then yes, we'll do that." Invariably, a request is then made to the borrower for additional documents (1 week for this step, 1 week total).

Step 3. The borrower gathers the additional documents and sends them in to bank (1 week for this step, 2 weeks total).

Step 4. The bank begins the underwriting process. The credit department enters the deal into its pricing model and gets a result that is below the hurdle. The lender goes back to borrower: "We can't do those terms. If the rate is *x*%, then we should be good." (2 weeks for this step, 4 weeks total).

Step 5. The borrower counters, and the "Let me check" process repeats. The deal goes back to the boss and the credit department, where they have to decide whether to take less or lose the deal. In this scenario they take less (which they usually do). The decision takes another two weeks (2 weeks for this step, 6 weeks total).

Step 6. Now the loan can go to committee for approval and full documentation before closing (4 weeks for this step, 10 weeks total).

In summation: It takes roughly 10 weeks to produce one below-target deal and one rocky relationship with a disgruntled borrower.

The New (Quick) Borrowing Process

Contrast that to the experience the borrower might have with one of the growing number of peer-to-peer lending companies out there, like Funding Circle. In a September 2014 article in *Entrepreneur* magazine[6], Funding Circle co-founder Sam Hodges claimed that "businesses can now apply for a loan in as little as 10 minutes and, if approved, receive funds in their account in less than two weeks."

---

[6]   Hodges, Sam. "Puncturing the 3 Newest Myths About Small Business Loans." Entrepreneur. N.p., 3 Sept. 2014. Web. 17 Feb. 2017. <https://www.entrepreneur.com/article/236996>.

Even if you assume that Hodges' estimate might be on the low side of actual turnaround times, there's a broad gap between two weeks and 10.

There are still multiple advantages that traditional banks enjoy over their peer-to-peer lending competitors. Bank rates are typically cheaper, and they bring an expertise to the table that peer-to-peer lenders can't match. While filling out an online application in the comfort of your home may sound nice, there's something to be said about getting the personal time and attention of a lender who can help walk you through the process and build an ongoing relationship with you.

There's a reason, however, why peer-to-peer lending is grabbing market share. Borrowers are often willing to overlook the disadvantages for the sake of a much faster loan process. On its site, Funding Circle features a case study[7] on the furniture company Yogibo, which used a Funding Circle loan to expand its operations.

"I had great opportunities to grow our business that I just couldn't miss out on," Yogibo founder Eyal Levy told Funding Circle. "So I looked for a lender that was ready to think creatively and make quick decisions."

It's imperative then that banks take steps to shorten their lending timelines and to be more creative with the options they offer borrowers. To do that, they must move the pricing process from the back of the bank to the front.

The Siren Song of One More Report

The 1999 cult-classic movie *Office Space* really seemed to capture the frustration felt at businesses all across the country. Why did it resonate with so many? Perhaps because, as over the top as it tried to be, it somehow managed to land squarely in the realm of perfectly realistic. Like this famous scene:

---

[7] "Yogibo review - selling comfort for plush profits." Funding Circle US. N.p., 16 July 2015. Web. 17 Feb. 2017. <https://www.fundingcircle.com/us/resources/yogibo/>.

Bill Lumbergh: Hello, Peter. What's happening? Uh . . . we have sort of a problem here. Yeah. You apparently didn't put one of the new coversheets on your TPS reports.

Peter Gibbons: Oh, yeah. I'm sorry about that. I, I forgot.

Bill Lumbergh: Mmmm . . . yeah. You see, we're putting the coversheets on all TPS

reports now before they go out. Did you see the memo about this?

Peter Gibbons: Yeah. Yeah. Yeah. I have the memo right here. I just, uh . . . forgot. But, uh, it's not shipping out till tomorrow, so there's no problem.

Bill Lumbergh: Yeah. If you could just go ahead and make sure you do that from now on, that will be great. And uh, I'll go ahead and make sure you get another copy of that memo. Mmmkay? Bye, bye, Peter.

Lenders watching that scene probably shook their heads ruefully and thought of their own version of the dreaded TPS report at their bank, something that the back of the bank keeps insisting on using but doesn't do anything to help lenders do their jobs.

That report has its roots in a common bank disconnect. When loan officers are sitting with the customer, battling the competition, trying to set customer expectations, and still secure good loans for the bank, every time they cross the finish line, it feels like a win. But when the loan committee sits to review the terms and sees the compromises made to land the business, the finish line seems nowhere close.

The prescription for shrinking that gap is often a detailed report that can be shown to the lender so they'll better "understand the nuances."

These reports are generated and used to "educate" lenders, an education that can feel like getting beaten over the head. In many cases, the report only increases resentment between the two sides and fails to change the behaviors that are causing the internal conflict.

In response, many banks continue their quixotic quest for the perfect report, the one that will finally close the gap and ensure that all the lenders' deals are up to the standards of the review committee. But that's not the issue. The problem isn't about what the report says. It's about *when* that information is being shared with the lenders.

> *"If you only have a hammer, you tend to see every problem as a nail." – Abraham Maslow*

Your Lenders Are Your Quarterbacks

Imagine you're the quarterback of your favorite football team. You run a series of plays—a couple of runs mixed in with a few passes—but are eventually stopped by the defense and are forced to punt.

You come over to the sidelines and sit on the bench in silence. No coaches come over to discuss strategy. No one calls down from the coaches' box above.

The same scenario unfolds time and again. You can't solve the riddle of the opposing defense and you're not getting any helpful feedback about what's happening. At halftime the coaching staff talks among itself while you sit and stew.

The second half is more of the same. It's not until afterward, when your team has struggled to score and you've absorbed another loss, that a coach approaches you. "Here's what happened," he explains. "And here's what you should have done."

You swallow down a string of expletives and resist the urge to stuff the coach into one of the nearby lockers. Instead, you keep your anger in check and state the obvious: "That's good to know. It would have been really helpful to have this information DURING THE GAME!"

Go ahead and chuckle at the absurdity of that scenario, but if you're a lender you're probably looking for a nearby wall against which to bang your head because for you, this scenario isn't absurd . . . it's the way many banks handle their reporting process.

The most successful banks are the ones that empower their lenders with knowledge they can use "in the moment," while they're actually pricing the deal.

To do that you need a communication system in which your lender is treated like a quarterback, and not the one in our previous absurd scenario. During a game, the quarterback is connected with an array of coaches—his position coach, the offensive coordinator, the head coach, etc. In particular, the quarterback is receiving information from the guys up in the coaches' box, where they can see the entire field.

For a lender, that would be like getting feedback during a deal from the CEO, the Chief Lending Officer, a credit analyst, and other key decision makers. Like the coaches up in the box, they're the ones who can see the big picture, your goals and your entire portfolio.

Obviously, you can't have all those people at the table for every single loan deal. But you can give the lender feedback much further upstream than the dreaded after-the-fact reports they're now receiving. Ask your lenders what type of tools they need to win more deals and build stronger relationships while they do it. Then compare their answers to the tools you've put in front of them.

Are those tools empowering your lenders? Or just second-guessing them?

Hopefully you have the former. But even if you do, there's more. It's not enough to simply give your lenders the right pricing tools. You also have to trust they'll use those tools correctly.

Be Like Wooden: Try a Little Trust

John Wooden is arguably the greatest coach in basketball history. There's certainly no debate that he's at least on the short list. At UCLA, Wooden presided over a college basketball dynasty that likely will never be equaled, leading the Bruins to an astounding 10 national titles in 12 years, including seven in a row from 1967 to 1973.

But Wooden's impact went beyond just the college basketball record books. He was an endless font of inspirational quotes, and his views on leadership and teamwork—particularly his Pyramid of Success—resonated in the business world. We could go on and on about Wooden's accomplishments, but for bankers perhaps the most important thing about Wooden is what he didn't do.

Watch any televised basketball game today and you'll notice that the cameras spend almost as much time trained on the coaches as they do on the on-court action. Every few seconds coaches are up off the bench, shouting instructions at players, badgering officials, or trying to get the attention of either.

Watch some old film of Wooden during a game and you'll wonder if the video feed was frozen. The vast majority of the time he remained seated on the bench. While he consulted with assistants during the game and instructed players during timeouts, Wooden spent much of the time simply observing while the action unfolded.

"Don't look over at me," he would sometimes tell his players. "I prepared you during the week. Now do your job."

Wooden believed very strongly that the principal purpose of the coach was to get his team ready for the game. If the coach performed his job correctly, then the players would have everything they needed to do their "job" during the game. To Wooden, the players were the ones best suited to make decisions within the flow of the game because they were the ones on the court and in the midst of the action. If they felt trusted and empowered by their coach, they would be loose and confident and thus perform much better.

Contrast that view with coaches who attempt to control every aspect of the game as it unfolds. You know the type: they're the ones who insist the point guard look over to the sideline before every offensive possession. They give each player a set role and demand they stay within it. Players who fail to follow those guidelines quickly find themselves headed to the bench. These coaches are all about avoiding mistakes instead of creating opportunities.

That approach does often limit the number of errors, but it can also lead to players who no longer use their instincts on the floor. Instead, they look for approval from the bench before every key move they make, or they simply stop making decisions for fear of being wrong and getting pulled from the game.

How do your lenders perform when they're attempting to make a deal with borrowers? Do they have to "check with management" before trying something beyond just adjusting the rate? Or do they simply say no to deals that don't fit within their pre-set instructions?

Is that how you want your lenders to do their jobs? Or would you rather they analyze the situation and make adjustments to the deal, confident that the decisions they're making will help both the bank and their customer?

Who wouldn't want Door No. 2 in those scenarios? But to do that, you've got to channel the bank's inner Wooden. You've already prepared your lenders by giving them what they need to make decisions within the flow of the deal. Now you need to step back and let your lenders use those tools when it matters most.

It's not an easy thing to do. There's a reason why so many coaches would rather stalk the sidelines and shout instructions than sit on the bench and put the team's fate on the shoulders of their players.

But there's also a reason why the wall outside UCLA's locker room is covered with national championship banners.

Wait a Second . . .

After reading those last two sections, you may be saying something like this:

"Wait a second . . . . Isn't this a contradiction? First you told me that my lenders need more input during the course of the deal. But then you told me I need to back off and let them handle the deal themselves. Which is it?"

It's both, but we understand the confusion. Here's another way of thinking about it, while continuing to lean hard on the sports analogies.

During that hypothetical football game, you want information from your coaches, but, as the quarterback, you're still the one who has to figure out what to do with that feedback. You still have to decide whether to call the main play or change to an audible, and then, after the ball is snapped, you have to figure out which receiver should get your pass.

You don't want to be out there on the field without any information and feedback from your coaches. But you also know you can't hike the ball and then turn to the sidelines to get approval for what to do next. The defense doesn't have that sort of patience. Neither do potential customers, when you're trying to negotiate a deal.

The Bank Loan Process, Take Two

Let's go back now to our original hypothetical borrower scenario, but let's change some

things around using the lessons of this chapter.

Step 1. The borrower comes in for a loan. The lender quotes a rate and the borrower comes back with something different. The lender checks his pricing tool to see if the borrower's loan terms would reach the bank's targets.

Step 2. The tool lets the lender know that the borrower's proposal won't hurdle. "Let's see what we can do," the lender replies. "Tell me more about what you're looking for in this loan."

Step 3. The lender finds out that while the rate is important to the borrower, the borrower isn't terribly concerned whether the loan is for 60 months or, say, 57. The lender adjusts the deal using the shorter term and finds that it now meets the bank's target (Steps 1–3 occur within one conversation, 1 day total).

Step 4. The deal goes through to underwriting, where it passes with flying colors (2 weeks for this step, 2 weeks and 1 day total).

Step 5. The loan goes to committee for final approval. This step is now shortened because the deal won't have to be run through a model and the committee won't have to analyze multiple structures because the customer will have already worked through that with the lender (3 weeks for this step, 5 weeks and 1 day total).

In this revised version of the borrower's bank experience, the loan process takes five fewer weeks and many, many fewer headaches. The borrower comes away feeling better about the deal, as does the bank. And the lender comes away feeling like he can do his job, and do it well. A solid foundation is laid for what should be a lasting relationship between customer and bank.

You can see then why the pricing process benefits from moving forward, to the front of the bank. But that's obviously much easier said than done. Who would oversee that sort of transformation? Who would allay the fears emanating from the back of the bank, where they fret about what will happen when they no longer have absolute control over each deal?

CHAPTER 5: THE CASE FOR THE CHIEF PRICING OFFICER

> To do pricing right, you have to able to change it quickly. When's the last time you used "committee" and "quickly" in the same sentence?

B anks have chief executive officers, chief financial officers, chief investment officers, chief loan officers, chief information officers, chief marketing officers, and chief risk officers. But for some reason, there's no chief pricing officer.

There really should be.

Pricing is Difficult; Someone Needs to Own It

In Chapter 1, we laid out our arguments for why pricing may be the most important function that happens in a bank on a daily basis—the biggest indicator that you're building relationships that will fuel the bank's success. Yet in most banks, no one person really "owns" the pricing process.

Pricing is inherently a difficult task. It's a delicate balance between controlling volume, risk, and profitability. That in itself would be problematic, but then there's the matter of managing pricing across multiple parts of the balance sheet. In banks, multiple parts of the balance sheet means crossing departments.

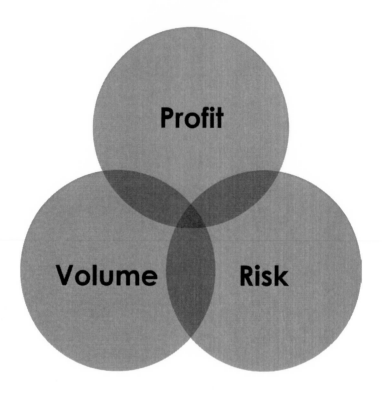

Pricing should be the front-end filter, where you can determine how many deals you get, at what level of risk, and for how much profit. It's the one place where you can dial in those growth/risk/profit levels to match the bank's high-level strategy.

Pricing is the one tactic that can be controlled, but banks rarely have any one person in charge of it. Instead, each of the various departments—lending, credit, deposits, etc.—has its own seat at the pricing table, and each may have conflicting goals that aren't in sync with the overall institutional strategy.

Take the case of deposits during the financial crisis. It was a period of time in which banks were almost drowning in liquidity; fear in the marketplace was leading people to park their money in the banking system, where banks then had to figure out what to do with it.

That was just fine for those on the deposit side, where they were customarily rewarded for growth. But on the asset side, there wasn't enough loan demand. That led to banks putting those funds in places that had nearly a zero yield. Between acquisition costs and interest expenses, banks were often putting dollars out at a negative carry.

That sounds obviously wrong-headed, but it was a hard process to alter. It would have required someone to urge the deposit folks to stop doing what they're rewarded to do and to turn off the deposit spigot.

Even if a bank has a solid ALCO group and can make and coordinate allocation decisions, problems can crop up at the next level—the tactical aspect of turning those decisions into real outcomes. This is where many banks break down, including our old friends from Chapter 2 and Chapter 3, Frankenstein Bank.

Frankenstein Bank was beset by departmental turf wars when it came to pricing. The stakeholders charged with finding a way to reach Frankenstein's balance sheet goals had different perspectives, but the same relative positions on the bank organizational charts. Lending and Finance continually butted heads, to the point where the person from Lending eventually left the bank in frustration. At that point Finance took over pricing and began handling it in a way that pleased Finance and no one else, focusing only on the price setting and not the price getting.

> *"Pricing pressures right now are incredible. The ability to effectively manage pricing will determine the survivors."*
> *— President of Dan Martin's Bank*

To avoid these sorts of scenarios, banks need a way to make sure all their department goals are aligned throughout the process, from coordinating the balance sheet through to setting and getting the prices. More to the point, they need a person responsible for handling that task.

That person is the Chief Pricing Officer.

What Does a Chief Pricing Officer Do?

If you're arguing for the creation of a Chief Pricing Officer (CPO) position, you'll need to go beyond the theoretical and into the actual job description. Here are the four main to-do's for the CPO.

1. Evaluate current position: Where does the bank stand? This isn't about individual portfolios or which group has which growth rate. This is about getting a clear picture of the bank's overall mix: Which assets are where? What yields are we getting? What are the durations?

2. Compare current position with future aspirations: Where would the bank like to be in terms of its asset/liability mix and the returns it's getting? How far does the bank have to go to get there?

3. Move the bank from No. 1 to No. 2: Once you know where things stand, aligning the pricing will help the bank make that shift, but only if there's commitment to the process. That can only happen if the CPO breaks down the walls between the various silos to make sure the bank is consistent, both in the decisions it makes and in the data it uses to make those decisions.

4. Measure and adjust: This doesn't happen if you only discuss pricing once a quarter or in ALCO meetings. Aligning your pricing tactics to match the bank's overall strategy is not a "set it and forget it" thing. Effective CPOs constantly work to make sure they get the right data in the hands of the right people, the ones who are doing the producing. For example, the folks on the deposit side would have direction about whether they need to slow down their intake; on the lending side, lenders would have information about which types of deals the bank needs to be pursuing and which categories are nearing saturation. Again, this information needs to be shared

at the right time, not after the fact. (Remember our quarterback analogy from Chapter 3.)

Why Not a Committee?

Let's say you've sold the stakeholders on the idea of a Chief Pricing Officer, and you've explained what the CPO will do. Chances are high you'll then get this question: "Why should one person have all this power? Wouldn't it be better to have a committee make this decision?"

Certainly a committee is better than nothing. Getting representation from the different areas of the bank will improve your pricing consistency. But ask yourself this: How many committees in your bank are really that effective in getting things done?

To get pricing right, you have to able to change it quickly. You need to make fast decisions, to be able to look at the current situation, and make the right adjustments to keep the bank moving from where it currently stands to where you want it to be. Take too long to deliberate and the land-scape will have already shifted by the time you put your tactics in motion.

Accountability is also critical. From a numbers standpoint it's pretty easy to track, like watching a progress bar fill up on a software download. To hold someone accountable, however, it needs to be "someone" and not "some group."

Who Is Your Chief Pricing Officer?

Congrats! You've made it this far! You've gotten buy-in from the powers that be to create the Chief Pricing Officer position and on what the CPO's job description should be.

The next hurdle is figuring out who should fill this critical role.

First, you don't necessarily have to add to headcount for this, or look outside the bank. This is key because many banks are likely to push back at the idea of hiring another C-level executive. You can probably find the person you need within your current organization.

The person needs to have enough of a finance background to do the heavy lifting when it comes to finding the right metrics and the right data because you'll be measuring risk in a system separate from where you'll be tracking production. You'll need someone with the technical skills to align those types of things.

The CPO candidate will also need to have authority within the organization. This person is going to be coming into a lot of personal fiefdoms within the bank and moving things around to make sure everything matches up and aligns. When they make a change in pricing, the senior lenders should feel compelled to go along with the shift. That's not going to happen if the CPO is a junior-level employee. Again, pricing is probably the most important tactic you have, so the CPO's level of authority should match that.

Some of that authority comes from the CPO's position in the bank, but some of it should come from the CPO's personality and approach to the job. He or she needs to have the power to enact change across a disparate collection of groups and goals, but will also need the finesse to ensure that this feels more like a collaboration than a dictatorship.

Finally, the CPO will need friends in high places. When companies try something new, the key players always look for signals from upper management. If that group is silent and passive, then it sends the message that the change is simply the flavor of the month; those who disagree or don't want to change can just be patient and passive and things will eventually return to the way they were. But if the powers that be demonstrate strong backing for something like the CPO concept, it lets everyone know that they need to get on board with what's happening, like it or not.

Even if you get to this point you may still need one more thing to make your case for a Chief Pricing Officer: a real-life success story.

Don't worry, we've got that covered.

The Dan Martin Story

Dan Martin has worked at the same Midwestern bank for his entire career, working his way up from his early days as teller into a management position as a profitability analyst. He is a self-described "finance" nerd who loves Excel and has spent years familiarizing himself with the ins and outs of pricing. Eventually Dan came to the realization that the tool the bank's lenders were using to price loans, a funding rate sheet, simply wasn't up to the task.

"A lender would just be tasked to say 'Hey, you need a certain spread on top of that.' It was pretty easy," Dan recalled. "Which is probably why the lenders also liked it. We all like simple things. But a lot of the decisions weren't necessarily good ones."

Dan set about creating a better tool, an Excel spreadsheet that could link with other databases and quickly crunch the numbers when a lender created a certain scenario, thus helping the bank price better deals. Once he had a base model in place, Dan made continuous improvements to it, expanding its flexibility and versatility.

Here is where we reach two of the key points in Dan's story.

First, while Dan had the finance background that is a key part of the CPO position, he also had experience working in customer-facing jobs. Dan recognized the need for what he called "a consultative approach" to pricing deals. He believed that when a lender sat down with a borrower, the lender should "think of five different ways to skin the cat, instead of just, 'This is what they asked for.'"

Even though Dan tried to put himself in the shoes of the lenders, it took quite a while before he got widespread buy-in for his pricing model. He experienced plenty of pushback from lenders who wanted to keep doing things the way they already knew.

"I remember banging my head against the wall so many days of those years, saying to myself, 'This is so much easier.'"

This brings us to the second important point: It wasn't enough that Dan's model was an improvement. He needed backing from the executive level.

The breakthrough came when the Chief Lending Officer in Dan's region mandated that information from Dan's pricing model had to be included in every packet.

"Once he gave that blessing, that's when they had to use it," Dan recalled.

The model produced results at the regional level, and when Dan was moved to the bank's central headquarters, his creation became the subject of intense interest.

"Within a few weeks I was in a room with execs I'd only heard of but had never met," he said. "They looked at the model and said, 'Man, that's good. That's way better than what we're doing right now.'"

Within three months of arriving at headquarters, Dan was moved from a job in which he dealt with budgeting and forecasting into one in which his focus was purely pricing.

"They were able to change my job into something I was really more passionate about," he said. "Kudos to them."

The bank was essentially checking off each box in the "Who Should Be Your Chief Pricing Officer?" checklist. In Dan they had someone with a finance background who also understood the importance of the lender/borrower relationship. They'd backed his ideas and put him in a position of authority to ensure his tactics would be carried out. By putting Dan in charge of a pricing overhaul for the entire bank, they also put the accountability squarely on his shoulders.

Dan did not disappoint. He quickly realized that his homegrown tool would not scale beyond the regional level and went shopping for something that could be managed across multiple regions and would integrate with the bank's customer relationship management (CRM) and other software systems. When he found the right software, he told his bosses, "If I could build anything, it would be this."

This is another point at which Dan's CPO story could have been derailed. The bank could have looked at the price tag and opted to spend less money on a project that was, to borrow from the Stephen Covey example in Chapter 1, basically "sand." Thankfully, the president of Dan's bank knew full well what a huge rock pricing was.

"Pricing pressures right now are incredible," the president said then. "Over the next few years it will only intensify. The ability to effectively manage pricing will determine the survivors."

Dan's bank purchased the pricing software he had requested, and they made him the Director of Pricing Strategy and Performance. In the past two years, the bank has not only survived but has also thrived.

Before implementing the pricing software companywide in the second quarter of 2013, the bank's NIM had underperformed its peer group (as defined by S&P Global) by 23 basis points. During the two years after implementation, the pendulum swung completely in the opposite direction, and Dan's bank produced a NIM that outperformed its peer groups by 11 basis points. For a bank of Dan's size, those 11 basis points translated to more than $17.2 million per year. Overall, the 34 basis point turnaround (from underperforming by 23 basis points to outperforming by 11 basis points) translated to more than $53.3 million per year.

Dan's pricing strategy has played a central role in his bank's success, but when he talks about it now, he stresses the relationship aspect of his job over the math.

"I call myself a chief customer officer, just because that's what I'm focused on. I'm always looking at what's best for the customer—and the bank, obviously—and incorporating that into their experience."

The process of doing this brings Dan into contact with stakeholders across the full range of the bank.

"I'm constantly in front of these executives and cross-functional lines," Dan said. "I'm telling them about—and selling them on—the experience we now have for the bank, which for the first time is a consistent one across all our footprints. We don't step on each other's toes."

Dan is the hero of our story, but he'll be the first to tell you that he's had plenty of help along the way. A Chief Pricing Officer can align the bank's pricing tactics with its strategy, but there's still the critical matter of the people who actually "get" those prices: the lenders.

CHAPTER 6: WHAT MAKES A GREAT LENDER?

> Stop worrying about improving your worst lenders. Focus on empowering your best ones.

The banking industry is facing a crisis in the coming years.

We promise this isn't like the 10,001 articles you've already read about how banks are being "Uber-ized" by tech startups. We're talking about an entirely different problem. This problem is largely self-inflicted, given the cancellation of most in-house training programs, but it also should be solvable if we tackle it the right way.

The big crisis? Banks are short on new talent. They are especially lacking lending talent, and the shortfall is about to get much larger as the Baby Boomer generation retires with few qualified replacements in sight. Consider this sobering finding from Bank Director's 2016 Compensation Survey[8]: "Forty percent of survey respondents say that recruiting commercial lenders is a top challenge for 2016. When asked to describe their bank's efforts to attract and retain commercial lenders, 43% say there aren't enough talented commercial lenders. The same number say they're willing to pay highly to fill these valuable roles within their organization."

---

[8] McCormick, Emily. "2016 Compensation Survey: Where Are The Lenders?" Http://www.bankdirector.com/. N.p., 10 May 2016. Web. 17 Feb. 2017. <http://www.bankdirector.com/committees/compensation/2016-compensation-survey-where-are-lenders/>.

Why Your Best Lenders Matter More Than You Know

Every bank we've ever worked with has a huge variance in the level of lender production. The distribution typically looks like a power law curve, where the majority of production comes from a few big producers (which we call "Alpha Lenders"), while most of the headcount and cost comes from average and laggard lenders.

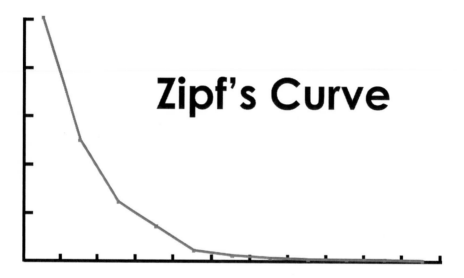

This is true of sales production in most industries, but it is especially important in banks. All of those deals live on the balance sheet, and their makeup dictates the bank's profitability and risk profile for years to come. Given that dynamic, the top lenders in a bank have a massive impact on the institution's performance. To get a sense of this, we must first take a detour and tell the story behind the "Zipf Curve."

In the mid-1930s, George Kinsley Zipf, a linguist at Harvard University, made the first of a series of fascinating discoveries. After tallying the frequency of word use in many different languages, Zipf noticed a nearly universal distribution. In almost all languages, the frequency of a word's use is inverse to its rank. The second most common word is used half as much as the most common word, and the tenth most common word is used one-tenth as much as the most common word. When plotted on a curve, it looks like this:

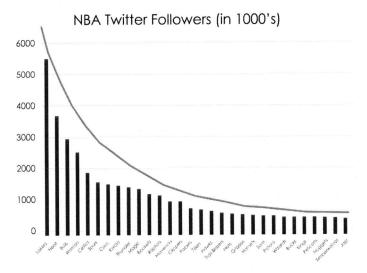

NBA Twitter Followers (in 1000's)

[9]

As Zipf dug deeper, he found that this power law curve applied to much more than language. It also applied to things like city populations, as the most populous city would be twice as big as the second largest city, and 100 times as big as the 100th largest city.

Interestingly, the distribution remained over time, so as the largest cities grew, the entire curve shifted. What started as a language phenomenon is now known as a Zipfian distribution, and it can be applied to far-ranging things such as the frequency of proteins in a genome sequence or even the number of Twitter likes for NBA teams.

How Zipf Applies to Your Bank

So what does this have to do with your lenders? In banking we often call this phenomenon the "80/20 rule," which is shorthand for the Pareto principle. (For you math nerds, a Zipfian distribution is just the discrete

---

[9]   https://www.theodysseyonline.com/2016-17-nba-twitter

version of the continuous Pareto distribution, so the two concepts are mathematical cousins, of sorts.)

We decided to dig into our client data at PrecisionLender to measure individual lender production. The more we played with this data, the more a familiar pattern started to emerge. First, we ranked all lenders that use our platform by portfolio size, and the result was a nearly perfect Zipfian distribution.

Much like individual books, though, individual banks also showed the same distribution. To the left is a detailed look at one bank. Its top lender has a portfolio balance over $200 million. Meanwhile, the average balance for all of the bank's lenders with a portfolio (49 in total) is $26 million.

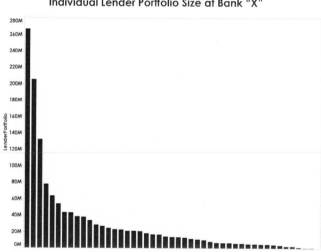

Individual Lender Portfolio Size at Bank "X"

This Zipfian data story repeated itself over and over among the banks we studied. All of them had just a few big producers at the top, while the rest of their lenders had relatively small portfolios.

(Bonus: If you produced a chart that lists those banks in order by their total loan portfolios it would create—you guessed it—a basic Zipfian distribution.)

Getting More From Your Best Lenders

While this was an interesting find, we initially thought of it as a classic "vanity metric," something interesting but without much value. As we discussed it with a few lenders from the top of those charts, however, that sentiment changed. In fact, it started to sound a lot like the venture capital business.

Fred Wilson, a well-known partner at the venture capital (VC) firm Union Square Ventures, published a great post called "Losing Money"[10] on his AVC.com blog. Here was the part that resonated:

> Our first USV fund, our 2004 vintage, has turned out to be the single best VC fund that I have ever been involved in. We made 21 investments. We made money on twelve of those investments. We lost money on nine of them. And we lost our entire investment on most of those nine failed investments. The reason that fund performed so well has pretty much nothing to do with the losses. It was all about five investments in which we made 115x, 82x, 68x, 30x, and 21x.

If you chart out the returns, there were a couple of massive homeruns, a few middling successes, and then a bunch of zeroes. Fred's point was that while the zeroes were valuable learning experiences, ALL OF THE PERFORMANCE came from the top of the curve, and his fund succeeded because they used time, money, and resources accordingly.

Loan portfolios in banks are built on similar distributions. (FYI, customer profitability also happens to follow a Zipfian distribution in most of the banks we checked.) Yet banks focus time, money, and resources at the exact other end of the curve from where Fred's firm put their focus.

---

[10]   Wilson, Fred. "AVC." Losing Money – AVC. N.p., 7 Apr. 2016. Web. 17 Feb. 2017. <http://avc.com/2016/04/losing-money/>.

In this case, we are not talking about loan losses. Those absolutely need time and attention. We're talking about all of the rules, systems, and management time put into "corralling" the bank's least productive lenders.

You can think of the Zipf curve like this. If a bank's top lender generates $1.00 of returns, then the fourth-best lender would generate $0.25, and the 100th best lender would generate $0.01. In other words, you have dollar lenders, quarter lenders, and so on, all the way down to your penny lenders.

The issue is that banks put rules in place to keep their penny lenders from making penny mistakes. As there are a lot more penny lenders, that takes a great deal of effort and resources from management. In addition, those rules do very little to help your dollar lenders. In fact, the rules put in place to keep penny lenders from making mistakes actually make it harder for your dollar lenders to be creative and responsive to their borrowers.

In our world of pricing, we see banks spend inordinate amounts of energy trying to avoid pricing exceptions for their penny lenders. "Don't do any loans over seven years. Don't do non-recourse loans under any circumstances. Don't offer ANY pricing below the hurdle rates."

This creates mountains of red tape that bog down dollar lenders trying to serve the bank's best clients. Philosophically, the bank would be willing to bend the rules and be responsive to its most important borrowers, but in reality, the structures set in place for the penny lenders make it very difficult to have that flexibility.

"Do your lenders have better tools for playing fantasy football than servicing their customers?"

Most banks admit that their lenders primarily use tools that are designed to "say no" to deals.

Think of it this way. Would it be easier to take a typical nickel lender, and double their production, or take a dollar lender, and make them a $1.05 producer? Also, if you want to move the needle on portfolio performance or asset mix, where are you more likely to make a dent? The focus should be at the top of the curve.

The Rising Tide Lifts All Boats

Do you want to know the really cool part? Remember from the growth of cities example that the distributions tend to remain intact. If you improve the performance at the top of the curve, the best lenders will produce a ton of business with your best customers. That generates goodwill and brand awareness that benefits the rest of your lenders. So as your top lenders get better, they don't actually put distance between themselves and everyone else. Instead, they lift the entire performance curve.

We've measured portfolio size, but what is the real impact of all of that production? To get to that number, we have to first identify the top producers—the "Alpha Lenders." There are lots of ways to define an Alpha Lender, but for consistency in this discussion we will keep it simple and use portfolio size as the determining factor. The average portfolio size is obviously different depending on the bank, as differing strategies create different loan mixes and organizational structures. So we used a measure of a lender's portfolio size relative to the other portfolios within their own bank.

In most of our client banks, the top 20% of commercial lenders produce the majority of the total commercial portfolio. The really impressive part, however, is that they not only produce more volume, they also produce more profitable deals as measured by risk adjusted ROE.

Take a look at this bank, a PrecisionLender client, which has close to 200 commercial lenders. We divided their lenders into deciles by portfolio size, and then compared the top few groups:

ROE	Top 20	21-40	41-60
Average	12.7%	9.8%	7.7%
Minimum	2.4%	-9.1%	-5.3%
Maximum	26.0%	22.3%	18.9%
Median	13.2%	9.3%	8.1%

Total Loan Volume	Top 20	21-40	41-60
Sum	3,018 M	1,166 M	518 M
Average	151 M	58 M	26 M
Minimum	80 M	37 M	17 M
Maximum	361 M	79 M	36 M
Median	139 M	57 M	26 M

The top 20 lenders have a median portfolio size of $139 million and generate median ROEs of 13.2%. Lenders 41–60 (solidly in the middle of the curve) have a median portfolio size of $26 million and median ROEs of 8.11%. That top group is allocating a giant chunk of the bank's capital, and is doing it more profitably than all of the other lenders. Wouldn't it be great to have more of those? How do we find or grow that kind of talent?

Then there's the question that keeps CEOs up at night: What happens if/when they leave? Answering those questions should be a top priority for bank management teams. The ones that get it right will be the big winners in the coming years. For those banks that don't get it right, our guess is they will be added to the growing M&A acquisitions stats, as they will have little choice but to sell before they lose too much ground.

Traits All Great Lenders Share

Because lenders allocate so much of the capital, their success (or lack thereof) will dictate the bank's profits and risk profile. Relying so heavily on just a few people tends to make CEOs nervous, though, and leads to a big underlying question. Are great lenders born, or are they made?

If great lenders are born, that is, they just happen to have innate abilities that others simply can't replicate, then the solution is simple: Start recruiting. This is expensive, and the results don't always live up to the expectations, but if great lenders are just born that way, then the only answer is to find proven producers and hire them away from the competition.

But what if great lenders are made? What if you can train and develop the next generation of stars from within your own ranks?

To see if this is possible, let's start by figuring out what makes some lenders great. What traits do they share that are so different from everyone else? We spend a lot of time talking to banks about this issue as we try to build platforms for the best lenders, and the same three traits come up over and over again.

Empathy (Embrace Your Inner Child)

First and foremost, lenders need to have empathy, and we mean empathy in the true sense of the word, not just the "suck up to the customer" approach that some banks teach. Empathy means that the lender starts the process with the customer and works backward into a viable deal. It can also mean acting like a five-year-old.

Child: Can I have ice cream for dinner?

Parent: No.

Child: Why?

71

Parent: Because ice cream isn't good for you.

Child: Why?

Parent: Because it has no nutritional value.

Child: Why?

Parent: Um, I guess because its makers wanted to make sure it was tasty.

Child: Why?

Parent: So they could sell more of it.

Child: Why?

If you're a parent, you know this conversation all too well. And if you're an honest parent, you know that at times all those incessant questions can be downright annoying. You also know that asking those questions is a critical part of the child's developmental process. Children have no built-in knowledge base, so asking questions—and getting answers—is the way in which they begin to make sense of the world around them.

It's similar to great lending, minus the "annoying" part.

Great lenders always ask the extra question to put themselves in their borrower's shoes. They know that the more knowledge they can gather about the customer's situation, the more ways they can find to structure a deal that will benefit both the borrower and the bank.

What kind of project are they financing? How will it affect the rest of their business? Which deal terms are likely to be most painful to them, and which are deal killers if we don't get them right? Empathetic lenders never start from a standard structure on a rate sheet. Making it fit into the bank's policies and profitability targets comes later, after they have established what works best for the customer.

It's also not enough to just fire away with question after question. Great lenders listen—really listen—to the answers their customers give. That may sound simple, but if you've ever watched a locker room interview scrum after a big game, you'll see how often people who are paid to ask questions fail to do this.

Sports reporter: Johnny, tell us about your game-winning hit.

Player: Well, I was just looking for a pitch to drive. But I really think the key was the week I spent in a sweat lodge before the game. That really cleared my mind.

Sports reporter: Uh huh. So what are your thoughts about tomorrow's matchup?

We exaggerate here to make a point. Some sports reporters are so intent on getting through their list of questions (and getting back to the press box to file a story before deadline) that they fail to listen to answers that, if they followed up on them, would give them a much better story.

How would this play out in a lender/borrower interaction? Consider this hypothetical situation we often use when demonstrating the PrecisionLender software.

Let's say you're trying to win a deal with a borrower for a $1-million commercial real estate loan. During the loan process, the borrower says he's planning to go with Bank Down The Street, which is offering a rate that's 50 basis points lower.

Some lenders throw up their hands right then and there. The deal doesn't fit their rate sheet, so, oh well. They don't look for alternate ways to get the deal done. Empathetic lenders start asking questions. "What can you tell me about this deal?"

Perhaps then you find out how Bank Down The Street is offering such a low rate. Maybe it's because part of the loan is guaranteed. That could be the end of the story. Great lenders, however, channel their inner annoying child and ask about the guarantee: Who's providing it? What are the details?

In this hypothetical, the guarantor is the borrower's father-in-law. Again, this could be the end of the line, but the empathetic lender, unlike the mediocre sportswriter, is listening to the answer, and he detects that the borrower is less than thrilled at the prospect of "owing one" to his father-in-law. So the lender asks more questions and finds out that the borrower would be more than willing to cut a few months off the maturity of the loan if it means he can get the same low rate and not have to rely on his father-in-law's guarantee.

By asking questions and listening to the answers, the empathetic lender has gathered enough information to turn the tables and win another deal for his bank. In the end, the only people truly annoyed are the lenders working at Bank Down The Street.

There is another side to empathy, as well. The best lenders know that getting a deal done quickly and efficiently relies on a lot of other people. Along the way they might need help from loan assistants, credit analysts, appraisers, attorneys, board members, title companies, and branch staff, just to name a few. Lenders might be able to steamroll those folks to get what they need once or twice, but to be able to consistently get complex transactions done, they will need to show noticeable empathy and respect for everyone involved.

Communication Skills

The second trait is related to the first. Part of empathizing with a borrower is understanding that while you may be neck-deep in multi-million dollar loan transactions every day, this is a rare event for customers. Lenders need to be great communicators who can clearly spell out what the process will look like from the beginning, including the big milestones and potential risks. Then, the borrower needs regular updates on progress, even if you are still just waiting for appraisals, title work, or approvals. Put yourself in your borrower's shoes. They are waiting for you to get some mysterious behind-the-scenes paperwork done so they can get the capital they need. Delays (or denials) mean dead projects and lost money, so going weeks without hearing anything will inevitably lead to frustration.

Dallas's grandfather was a construction foreman for large government and commercial projects. He was essentially a project manager, ensuring that all of the various crews and sub-contractors got their piece of the job done on time, in the right order, and up to standard. He described it slightly differently: "I basically herd cats through a hailstorm."

Each project would have unique parameters and would require coordination between the customer (usually a developer), the foreman's bosses (the general contractor), and all of the various work crews for the general and sub-contractors. The day-to-day work was largely walking around the job site, inspecting progress, and then communicating that progress to the affected parties. It was essential that the framing crew knew exactly when the foundation crew would be done so they could have the right materials on hand and be ready to start as soon as they finished. The electricians needed to know where the plumbing would go, and when the HVAC crew would be there. And the bosses always needed to know what was late, how far over budget they were, and who was to blame.

That job function probably sounds familiar to a commercial lender. In a typical commercial loan transaction, there is a similarly large group of involved parties. There is a borrower, who will typically have partners, staff, attorneys, and possibly consultants working on the deal. If you are financing a purchase, you will have contingents from the sellers and brokers, as well. On the bank's side you will have senior lenders, loan assistants, credit analysts, the finance team (for pricing), and approval committees.

And of course you have the litany of third-party service providers for appraisals, environmental studies, document prep and review, collateral inspections, and title work. A good commercial lender jumps into the fray and helps coordinate all of these parties, each of whom has their own perspective and agenda in a multi-million dollar transaction.

A mistake can be disastrous for anyone involved. Sounds a bit like herding cats through a hailstorm, doesn't it?

The best lenders do a masterful job of communicating with everyone involved, just like it's a construction job site. The credit team knows when the appraiser will be finished, and the customer knows what happens if the number is less than expected. The attorneys are notified when the title work is complete and the documents can be prepared. The customer and the bosses are always aware of what is late, how far away from budget the process is, and who is to blame.

Bank management teams need to facilitate this process instead of just hoping the lenders figure it out. Since much of the job is really "deal choreography," lenders should get formal training on project management and communication. Just as important, the bank should invest in some basic tools to help lenders keep all of the balls in the air.

Even if you don't have a full-blown customer relationship management (CRM) or project management system, there are lots of easy-to-use and inexpensive software as a service (SaaS) products that can be used for these purposes. Regardless of the solution you choose, just make sure you aren't sending your lenders to a gun fight with a knife because the big guys are starting to make large investments that will significantly outclass the legal pads and sticky notes you're using now.

Quantitative > Qualitative (Avoiding "Tilt")

When Dallas was learning the banking business, one of his early bosses taught him something really important. He said, "If you stay in this business long enough, you will eventually get burned by every type of borrower. Learn your lessons, but don't let it get emotional." Put another way, when you're a lender, you need to avoid "tilt." If you've ever played poker, you know all about "tilt."

The phrase comes from the warning sign on pinball machines that lit up whenever a player tried to "tilt" the machine to get the ball to move a certain way. In other words, it's a pithy way of saying "off balance." A player goes on "tilt" when he's overreacting to the results of previous hands, and he is now letting that emotion dictate his moves. His decision making has lost all balance. It's a condition that's not unique to the poker table. It also affects lenders.

What are the different types of tilt? An article at pokerology.com describes six forms, several of which may look familiar to lenders:

Berserker Tilt: The most common type, this is the guy who's had a stretch of bad luck, or has perhaps lost a hand to someone who made all the wrong moves but somehow won the pot anyway. Now the Berserker is frustrated and playing far too aggressively. He's mad and gosh darn it, he's going to get all his money back NOW.

Berserker Tilt (Lending version): Lose a couple of deals to Bank Down the Street and you can find yourself in "Berserker" mode, hell-bent on winning the next one, even if the logical part of your brain is desperately trying to tell you that the numbers don't add up.

Lily-Liver Tilt: This poor guy lost a really brutal hand—maybe his full house was beaten by a better full house, or his king-high flush was bested by an ace-high flush. The Lily-Liver now sees losses around every corner. He's playing scared, folding every hand unless absolutely certain he has a winner (and it almost never is).

Lily-Liver Tile (Lending Version): You got burned by a deal that was structured well but went south later through no fault of your own. Now you're in "Lily-Liver" mode, avoiding making those deals, even though there's sound reasoning to do just the opposite.

Winner's Tilt: Proof that tilt isn't always brought on by losses, this player's won a few hands and suddenly he thinks he's invincible. Most likely he has confused luck with skill and thinks he had something to do with the dealer giving him just the card he needed. So, in future hands, he'll ignore all the warning signs and just keep betting because past results tell him HE IS THE MAN!

Winner's Tilt (Lending version): You've brought in some deals with shaky fundamentals and they actually worked out in the end. Now you're on "Winner's Tilt" and you've mistakenly decided that this is a viable formula going forward.

Frustration Tilt: This poker emotional state is brought on by, well, nothing. The player hasn't had any cards to play all night so finally he just decides, "To heck with it, let's make something happen!" That approach does indeed "make something happen" . . . it's just usually not something good.

Frustration Tilt (Lending version): It's a slow time in your market, so you decide to force the action. You offer loans at significantly lower rates, or you close deals with higher risk ratings, because hey, shaky deals are better than no deals, right? And maybe enough of those shaky deals will hold up to make your gamble pay off, right . . . RIGHT?!?!

These are all, of course, terrible ways to play poker and terrible ways to make loans. Every semi-serious poker player understands the basic rules of probability—that the outcomes of previous hands have no statistical relation to what will happen in the present hand (or in the hands after that.) The "Tilt Guy" is attempting to defy those rules, and it almost always ends badly for him.

The best lenders know to rely on the data and to ignore their "lizard brain," which falls for patterns that don't exist and attributes skill or risk to random wins and losses. Bankers who let their lizard brain call the shots often say things like "Remember that hotel deal from a few years back? We're NEVER doing another one."

The data and analytics will tell the best lenders which deals and structures are right. We've met lots of bankers who claim they are successful because they follow a "gut instinct." In our experience, they eventually find heartburn, either in the form of unforeseen risk or missed opportunities.

While there are lots of other traits that are important to being a successful lender, most of them will fall into one of those three buckets:

empathy, communication, and quantitative > qualitative. The one thing that you might have noticed is missing, though, is "technical knowledge." Don't lenders need to understand credit risk and the basics of how to structure a deal?

Absolutely, but we have also found that those skills don't make a great lender. They're table stakes—in other words, you have to have them to even play the game. Most banks we talk to are concerned about how to train the next generation of lenders, but the focus is almost always on credit training. Instead it should be on building relationships and adding value for customers. Teach lenders those skills, and big production will follow.

Developing the Traits: The Saga of Dave and Mike

Back in Dallas's early banking days, he worked with a couple of "star" lenders. One was a guy named Dave, a big-producing CRE lender. The other, Mike, was a younger guy who happened to work for Dave. The two had very different approaches—Dave was aggressive and an extrovert, while Mike was quiet and steady—but both got results. Eventually they both left for greener pastures, and that is where the story gets really interesting.

Mike jumped to a competing bank, and was able to take a surprisingly big chunk of his book of business with him. Over the last decade Mike has been promoted multiple times, and is now successfully leading and growing a new market for the bank.

Dave went to work for a smaller bank, becoming the CLO and a member of the executive management team. When Dave's old customers found they couldn't replicate their previous relationship with Dave at his new bank, they declined to follow him. Dave clashed with the management style of his new employers, and in just over a year, he was out of a job.

By any metric, both Dave and Mike had been very good lenders who seemed poised for big things. They each possessed the three big traits that we see in great lenders. Yet only one achieved "Alpha Lender" status.

Why did their career paths diverge? Because only Mike's bank took an active role in further developing those key traits.

Here are a few ways your bank can produce its own share of "Mikes."

Put Empathy into Action

Yes, some people simply have more empathy woven into their DNA, and you should seek out those types to be your lenders. Hiring absolutely matters. But a great lender has to be able to do more than just feel empathetic toward their borrowers; they have to be able to act on that empathy. This requires a specific environment at the bank that can serve as the foundation for differentiated service and better relationships.

While culture change is admittedly very hard, especially in large, complex organizations like banks, we often see commercial loan teams that develop their own distinct "mini-culture" that is quite different from the rest of the bank. Leaders of loan teams can absolutely create these mini-cultures and should strive for an environment that includes these core elements:

A Customer-Centric Approach

This doesn't mean "the customer is always right" and that you just bend to their demands. That is generally a bad idea in commercial lending. Instead this means that all interactions are designed to start with the customer and then work back from there to the bank. Set up the entire process so you can understand their needs, be flexible enough to meet them when possible, and respond quickly and efficiently.

Lenders Have Both Authority and Accountability

To be responsive to their customers, lenders must have the authority to make decisions. Obviously lenders should not have full autonomy in approving their own credits, but they should have the ability to make some basic decisions. This includes things such as loan structures, pricing, and renewal negotiations. For this to work, lenders must have clear guidelines and accountability for their results.

When banks get this right, they help lenders build deep, value-added relationships with their borrowers.

Transparency

Lenders are too often kept in the dark about the big-picture strategy of the bank. Why are loan goals set where they are? Which loan types fit best with the balance sheet? If lenders are expected to always act in the best interest of the organization, it's vital that they have a better understanding of where the bank is headed and how their contributions fit.

Communication Training

Having an open and ongoing dialogue with customers is essential for great lenders. However, very few banks actually train on these skills. If you mention "lender training" to bankers, they universally think of credit training. Yes, lenders need to understand the basics of credit so they know the difference between a good deal and a bad one, and know how to structure a deal that best fits the borrower's needs. But credit skills are, again, really just table stakes. We've seen plenty of folks with a great credit background who are terrible lenders.

To be able to communicate with customers, lenders also need an understanding of asset liability management. They must understand the why and the how behind the pricing differences for various structures. We have seen lenders be far more successful in selling floating rates or prepayment penalties when they understand the circumstances in which those structures matter most to pricing and can properly explain the details to their customers.

This falls into negotiating, which again, most banks ignore in training. Your lenders are negotiating millions of dollars in transactions for your most profitable and risky products. Why not get them formal training in negotiating a deal?

In addition, lenders need to be able to communicate deal progress to their borrowers. What steps still need to be completed? How long will it take? How can the lender help shepherd the deal through all of those steps so that closing happens when it is supposed to? Lenders should be able to answer all of those questions, which means dedicated training on "how the sausage is made."

Improve Your Lenders' Toolbox

Finally, lenders need to be able to overcome their lizard brain and make sound decisions based on data. These decisions include everything from how and where to prospect to where to look for likely credit problems in the existing portfolio. In short, lenders need to know what constitutes a good deal for the bank and should spend their time chasing those instead of pursuing deals that won't really move the needle.

To do this, though, lenders need better tools. We often ask the question, "Do your lenders have better tools for playing fantasy football than servicing their customers?" Most banks admit that their lenders primarily use software that is designed to "say no" to deals.

Risk management is important, but your lenders also need tools that help them "say yes" to deals and generate revenue. They need sales tools to help them prospect, price, and service their customers. Unfortunately, most walk into customer meetings armed with nothing to help but a pen and a legal pad.

Dave and Mike: Where Are They Now?

As you can see, with the right culture, training, and tools, the bank can have a great impact on the traits that make a great lender. Going back to Dave and Mike, those three things made all the difference in the outcomes.

Dave landed at a bank with an "old school" approach to banking, where lenders had no authority to serve customers, no training other than basic credit, and no tools outside of being able to look up customer balances on the core system.

Mike landed at a bank that was the polar opposite. The loan group put customers at the center of every decision, and they invested in the training and tools to develop great lenders. It certainly worked for Mike, and as we saw from the data on the profitability of Alpha Lenders, these are investments with a huge ROI.

CHAPTER 7: SUNLIGHT IS THE BEST DISINFECTANT

Choose transparency. When you give out information rather than hoarding it, you empower your lenders and gain the trust of your customers.

We've talked about how important the best lenders are and some of the characteristics they share. Very few bankers will challenge any of those concepts. But how do you make it hap- pen? How do you enable your lenders to be great? For many banks, the answer lies outside their comfort zone.

To be successful, banks must find ways to empower their lenders, giving them the freedom and autonomy—as well as the right tools—to make the necessary trade-offs and decisions quickly. It's not enough to just deliver valuable solutions. Lenders have to deliver them rapidly and in a way that builds trust with the customer at every point.

Providing value to the customers while still earning big returns for the bank is a tricky balancing act requiring a secret ingredient that may make banks cringe: transparency.

The Painful Story of Ryan

Ryan might just be the best illustration of why this secret ingredient is so critically important.

Ryan was the treasurer at his bank and a very, very bright guy. He understood the power of pricing. His problem was that he didn't think his lenders were very capable. He didn't trust them, so he tried to put strict limits on how much pricing information his lenders had access to. He wanted a bunch of progress reports that only he could see. Ryan was afraid that more data in the hands of lenders meant more chances they'd somehow muck things up.

As it turned out, things did go south, but not in the way that Ryan was trying so hard to avoid.

Instead, the lenders grew tired of trying to operate in the dark. They rebelled against management's pricing strategy, and blamed their lack of profitable production on Ryan.

Ryan's tale is, unfortunately, a fairly common one at banks. While Ryan did eventually come around—and his bank's performance rose as a result—going through those early struggles was a painful process for all involved.

It did, however, have a silver lining. It now serves as a cautionary tale that helps us make the case for transparency with our clients.

We touched on transparency briefly in Chapter 6, but we felt the topic was too important for just a passing reference. It deserves a chapter of its own, and it can be divided into two parts: transparency within the bank and transparency with the customer.

"Does the bank need to reach these targets because it's in trouble and it's trying to climb out of a hole? Or is it just getting greedy?

More than likely it's neither, but in the absence of information, you're probably jumping to one of those two conclusions.

Bank Transparency

Nature Abhors an Information Vacuum

We'll first address transparency within the bank. To do that, let's go back to Ryan's bank and take a walk in the shoes of his lending team. Let's say you've been given some aggressive ROE targets to meet and that those numbers represent a significant jump up from your previous targets.

- Why did the goals get pushed up so much? (You don't know because Ryan's not sharing that information.)

- How was the ROE target arrived at? Why that number? (You don't know because Ryan's not sharing that information.)

- Is anyone else struggling to meet these ROE targets, or is it just you? (You don't know because . . . you get the picture by now.)

Does the bank need to reach these targets because it's in trouble and it's trying to climb out of a hole? Or is it just getting greedy? More than likely it's neither, but in the absence of information, you're probably jumping to one of those two conclusions.

You can see how the atmosphere at Ryan's bank quickly became toxic, and how taking this approach nearly doomed Ryan's chances of getting his lenders to price and structure deals in a way that aligned with the bank's strategies. Worse than that, commercial lenders with little insight into the bank's strategies and even less authority were providing a terrible experience to their customers, who just happened to be the most profitable segment in the bank. The result: seven straight years of shrinking loan balances and profits well below their peer group.

How can your bank avoid those struggles? Instead of keeping your lenders in the dark, try a little sunlight instead.

Let There Be Light

Ryan's bank decided to make some wholesale changes to their lending process, including overhauls to pricing, underwriting, and lender incentives. This time, though, they decided to make transparency a guiding principle. The bank announced it was setting new, aggressive targets for its lenders for both growth and ROE. The management team held a meeting in which they walked the lending team through the numbers. They explained how the targets were determined and why they were set at those levels. They put the ROE into the bigger context of the bank so the lenders could understand how those targets fit into the overall direction for the institution. Just as important, they rolled out an impressive new integrated platform to help the lenders with the sales process.

Keeping Up with the Joneses

Everyone's performance was then put on display. Lenders could look at their own performances, but they also could see how each of their peers was doing. They could see how their boss was faring, and his boss, all the way up to how the bank as a whole was performing.

If they thought that the initial ROE target was nuts, they now had the facts that could either prove or disprove their assumptions. Without transparency, they likely would have just moved straight to, "These numbers are absurd." With transparency, they may still have concluded in a month or two that the goals were ludicrous, but as everyone in the bank had visibility into the results, they wouldn't have been alone in that conclusion and it wouldn't have been so hard to change direction.

Or they may just have discovered that most of the other lenders weren't having a problem with the new targets. Now they could see why the shift was made, and that they needed to get themselves in gear. A motivated lender is a better lender, and nothing motivates quite like good old-fashioned peer pressure. In fact, this bank went from a laggard to a market leader and grew loans by more than 40% during the two-year period following the change.

Meanwhile, as the bank transformed, so did Ryan. He has a newfound appreciation for working WITH his lenders instead of against them and has become one of his bank's most vocal advocates of transparency.

Going Granular

Transparency makes sense in managing and motivating lenders, but how does it translate to production? What do lenders at banks like Ryan's do differently to book more deals at higher profit levels?

We gained some valuable insight into this area when we researched how the best lenders at our client banks were performing. These top lenders were the beneficiaries of transparency. They'd been given clear targets and a clear understanding of all the terms in a deal. Then they were given the freedom to choose the path that would lead to a deal that satisfied the customer and met the bank's goals.

One example of this was in the area of rate granularity. We looked at how often lenders priced deals in quarter-percent rate increments (e.g., 3.25%, 4.75%, etc.) and how often they become more granular in their approach, opting for rates between the quarters instead (3.28%, 4.68%, etc.).

Rates on Non-Quarter Increments for Fixed-Rate Loans (Last 12 Months)

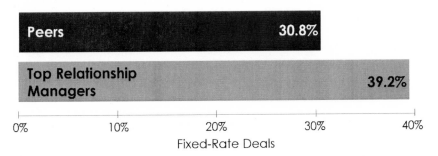

Focusing on fixed-rate loan originations from the last 12 months, we found that top lenders priced in non-quarter increments 27% more often than their lower-performing peers.

Those numbers had even more impact when we looked at the dollar amounts involved. Deals with non-quarter rates accounted for 64.7% of the top lenders' notional amounts on fixed-rate loans in the past 12 months, as compared to 46.2% for other lenders.

Notional Amounts on Non-Quarter Increments for Fixed-Rate Loans (Last 12 Months)

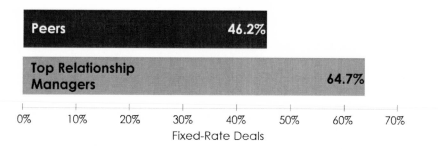

Put simply, top lenders priced on rates between the quarters more often, which allowed them to win much bigger deals.

This difference actually flies in the face of a lot of conventional wisdom in the industry. Many banks have trained their lenders to price on quarters and eighths, with the assumption being that if the real rate needed to make the deal "hurdle" on profitability is 4.18%, then rounding up to 4.25% will expand margins over time.

The reality, though, is that this tactic is rarely being used to round up a rate. Instead, lenders are looking at a competitive offer from the bank down the street and offering a rate that is the next rung down on the ladder. A competitive offer at 4.25% often means that a lender will offer 4.00% to win the deal. You can guess at the competitive reaction, which in part explains the multi-decade trend in net interest margin for the banking industry.

In contrast, the best lenders have a clearer picture of exactly where the line of profitability lies for any particular deal. Their banks have clearly communicated the targets, and thus the lenders know precisely where they stand for any rate, including those between the quarters.

In short, they know the value of every basis point, especially on larger deals. A basis point on their entire portfolio often translates to the annual salary of someone on their support staff.

Pricing between the quarters isn't just a way to add in the occasional basis point to help profits. It can also be a way to win a deal without having to jump all the way down to the next rung. If the real hurdle rate is 4.18%, and the competition is at 4.25%, why drop all the way to 4.00%? The bank can still undercut a competitor to win business, but it can be won without making the sacrifice too painful.

Rate granularity is a clear argument for why banks should practice transparency with their lenders. But what about being transparent with their customers?

Customer Transparency

Making "The Inside Deal" Just "The Deal"

> "You'll see. First they stick you with the undercoating, rust-proofing, dealer prep. Suddenly, you're on your back like a turtle."
>
> "Look at these salesmen. The only thing these guys fear is the walk-out. No matter what they say, you say, 'I'll walk out of here right now!'" — George Costanza, *Seinfeld*, "The Dealership"

George Costanza, Jerry Seinfeld's neurotic malcontent friend, uttered these two memorable lines during the Seinfeld episode that centered around Jerry's trip to the car dealership to buy a new Saab. Throughout, George constantly rails at Jerry to trust no one and to treat his deal negotiations with the salesman like a fight to the death. Jerry though, tells George to relax. The salesman, Puddy, is Elaine's boyfriend, so Jerry is going to get "the inside deal."

The episode works because George is in all his way-over-the-top glory, veins popping out of his forehead as he snaps at even the slightest hint of provocation. But it's also funny because Seinfeld's writers are tapping into something the audience feels as well: When you go to buy a car, you're not collaborating with the salesperson to reach a deal that pleases both sides. You're stepping into a battle, one in which the salesperson has more information and, thus, the upper hand.

But what if the salesperson voluntarily gave away some of that information and leveled the playing field? What if "the inside deal" was actually just a typical deal?

Transparency > Mystery

And what if commercial lenders took that approach?

Rather than drawing a line in the sand on rate and trying to make the customer blink, what if lenders opted instead for transparency over mystery and vulnerability over power?

Here's how that might work. A customer comes into the bank looking for a real estate loan at a specific rate. The lender plugs those numbers in and sees that the deal in that form won't reach his ROE target (transparency within the bank at work!), but he can see there are several other ways the deal can be adjusted so that it can work, with the rate the customer wants, perhaps by changing the rate type, or the length of the loan, the initial fees, etc.

Now for the crucial part: The lender then explains all this to the customer.

The lender opens himself up a bit, letting the customer "inside" and essentially giving a glimpse of what it's like on the lender side of the table. The customer doesn't have to guess at what the lender's goal might be. Instead, that information is out in the open, along with multiple ways in which the lender is willing to craft the deal.

Now the ball is in the customer's court, and they have a real voice in the pricing decision. Now that the lender has given a little, the customer is more likely to do the same, often by sharing some additional information that will help the lender create even more options that are suitable to both sides. The conversation changes from haggling over the bank's rates to an in-depth discussion of the borrower's business. What are their current struggles and future plans, and how can the bank best support them?

The alternative to that vulnerable approach is the power play, holding your cards close to the vest and waiting until the customer's need for capital overcomes his caution and discomfort. Sometimes that works, but sometimes, the customer pulls a Costanza and bolts for the door.

If your lenders open themselves up a bit, trust is built and the customer comes away feeling empowered. The lender comes away with a deal that meets targets and a customer who feels like they just got "the inside deal." That's a customer who's likely to bring more business to the bank in the future.

Caps and Floors

Let's take this concept of transparency with customers out of the hypothetical and into the practical.

Banks and their customers are both afraid of sudden changes in interest rates. Banks fear movement in either direction that might have a negative impact on net interest income, so they constantly try to match structures on the two sides of the balance sheet. That's Asset Liability Management 101, and it is manifested in pricing through higher rates for longer durations and an inherent preference for shorter, variable rate structures.

Customers fear sudden changes in rates for a much more direct reason; higher rates mean higher payments. This is most painful early in the loan, when the balance is highest. Customers aren't frightened that rates will go up steadily over time. What keeps them up at night is the prospect of rates suddenly shooting up the next day, leaving them in financial turmoil. Their response is a high demand for the certainty of longer terms and fixed-rate structures.

How do bankers reconcile this borrower demand for "cheap, fixed, and long" with the bank's preference to provide "expensive, variable, and short?" Most lenders seek the path of least resistance, avoiding conflict with their customers and offering the lowest rate and longest term they think their boss will allow. This is the path the entire industry has been on for years now, and it is exceptionally painful and risky given the current levels of interest rates.

The best lenders, on the other hand, have a very different solution for the same problem. They have a conversation with the customer, touching on the customer's fear of a rate spike, while also acknowledging the bank's need to have more NIM certainty. They often find a solution for both sides through the use of caps and floors.

When we looked at our data, we found that top-performing lenders offered variable-rate loans more often than their lower-performing peers (50% versus 39%). What's more, top lenders were *five times more likely* to use caps and floors on their variable rate deals.

Use of Caps and Floors on Variable-Rate Deals

By using a cap on a variable rate, lenders are able to provide the benefit of the lower rates at the short end of the curve while still providing risk mitigation to customers. Customers know the payments can only climb so high, but they don't have to pay the relatively expensive cost of a fixed rate loan to get that insurance. In exchange, most customers are willing to trade a floor on the rate as well. A floor comes with little additional cost to the customer, yet it helps the bank guarantee a minimum rate of earnings. The bank and the customer are able to share the interest rate risk in the most efficient way possible.

In addition to more effectively solving their customer's problem, these top-performing lenders were also able to generate superior returns for the bank. The deals they won that used caps and floors had an average ROE of 30%.

Why is this structure so profitable? The first reason is simple: supply and demand. If your competitors are all trying to offer the cheapest and longest fixed rate they can stomach, they will be battling in a race to the bottom. A variable rate with caps will have a lower nominal rate but still alleviate the customer's fear. It is not simply a commoditized offering that's the cheapest rate in town.

For the second reason we had to dig one level deeper in the data. The best lenders don't just book five times more caps and floors. Their cap/floor deals are one-fifth as long as the ones other lenders book.

Constructing shorter-term deals is a critical difference. This tactic allows the best lenders to utilize the structure of the deal to solve the borrower's problem in a way that is also beneficial to the bank. This balancing act hinges on the uncertainty surrounding forward interest rates and the volatility around possible future outcomes.

Specifically, the markets have a good idea about what short-term rates will look like in the near future, 3 months or even 2 years out. The uncertainty increases dramatically for a longer time horizon, however, such as five years out. Thus, banks can offer caps within a near-term window at a low cost, while longer-term protection becomes an expensive proposition.

The good news is that customers don't fear gradual increases five years from now because by that time the debt will have amortized down. Instead, customers fear the spike in the short term. A short-term cap allows customers to sleep soundly at night at almost no cost to the bank, providing the classic (but hard to find) win-win scenario in loan negotiations.

For lenders to be able to provide solutions like this, they must first be aware of their borrowers' fears and their unique situations. That requires a completely different kind of conversation, and it all starts with lenders being able to transparently show borrowers exactly where their deal stands relative to the bank's "line in the sand."

This kind of communication may border on blasphemy in many banks, but your customers are experiencing transparency now in all walks of life, from car buying to medical care choices. Heck, part of the appeal of mobile services like Uber is that you can see all parts of the transaction (cost, driver ratings, car type, even current location) before finalizing the deal.

How long will your customers put up with a bank that uses asymmetrical information to bully them in negotiations?

CHAPTER 8: BUILDING A PRICING ECOSYSTEM

Banks spend as much as 70% of their total technology budget on maintaining legacy systems, but that is not where value is created.

In Chapter 7, we told the story of Ryan, a bank treasurer who was reluctant to share information with his lenders. Ryan did eventually come around, and the bank's newfound transparency helped them become one of the top performing banks in the United States. This wasn't as simple as saying, "Let there be light!" A change of that magnitude in both culture and process is a daunting task to undertake. Sharing may be a lesson taught in kindergarten, but it's a skill that's often in short supply at large banks, leading to substantial roadblocks when attempting real transformation.

To solve this problem, Ryan's bank knew they needed to overhaul much of their organization, including people, processes, and much of their existing infrastructure. They began by hiring Dean to function as their Chief Pricing Officer.

Dean didn't jump right into the math of Price Setting. Instead, he led the systems overhaul that would enable the Price Getting. (See Chapter 2 and Chapter 3 for more on Price Setting and Price Getting.) Dean knew that establishing an efficient and transparent pricing process would require much more than just an update to the bank's dated pricing model. It meant building an entire pricing ecosystem.

What does a pricing ecosystem look like? To start, let's back up and take a look at the typical building blocks banks have in place.

The Heart Versus the Brain

How do banks really add value? How do they make money? Those questions should not only have easy answers, they should also be the driving force behind the bank's most important strategy decisions. So why aren't more banks pointing resources to the systems that help them get better at those two things?

The Heart

The answer, unfortunately, might just lie with the marketing genius who decided to name the bank's accounting software the "core system." Every bank we've ever talked to has a love/hate relationship with their "core system" and the vendor that supports it.

The issue is that banks are asking these systems to do things they were never designed to do. Core systems were built for debits and credits, making sure that everything balanced and no pennies were lost. They are the epitome of a commodity in the banking business in that there is really no way to differentiate based on them. Keeping track of transactions and balances is the absolute minimum requirement, and everyone ends up delivering the same end product to the customer (an accurate accounting of transactions).

So, yes, the core is vital, which is why it's called the "heart" of the bank. You have to have it, and its job is to circulate basic but essential elements to the other parts of the bank. It was not, however, designed to be a central data warehouse from which you can manage the bank.

The Brain

The brain is the collection of systems and processes where banks make decisions that generate real value and returns. Here's what it looks like when those tools are put to work closing a valuable deal.

Generally, the sales process is tracked in some sort of CRM system, you negotiate through a pricing and profitability tool, and then the deal runs through various workflow systems (underwriting, doc prep, etc.) to get to closing. After it is on the books, the same CRM and underwriting tools will be used to service and manage the loan, and you will use other portfolio-level resources to measure the profits and risk so that the bank can adjust strategy where necessary. Altogether, the systems will look something like this:

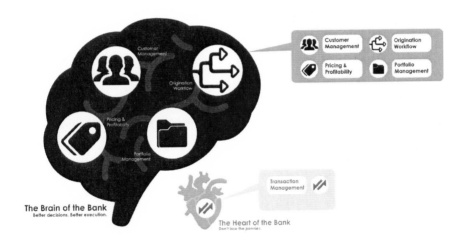

The brain is where banks build relationships with prospects and customers; it's where they analyze and price the risks they are taking, and it's the means by which banks can attentively service and support their customers once they are on the books. Those three functions are the only ways that banks truly differentiate themselves and generate value for all stakeholders.

When we walk through this "heart versus brain" layout with banks, they almost universally agree with the principals, including the argument that the brain is where they add value. Yet, if you compare the amount of resources allocated to each, including vendors and dedicated personnel, spending on the heart systems dwarfs the spending on the brain systems. This disconnect between cost and value is one of the roots of the industry's vulnerability to new competition and customer apathy.

So, how can bankers solve this problem? The answer is twofold.

First, they need to continue pushing back on their core vendors. The basic strategy employed by the vendors has been to make it so painful to switch that you will put up with the continued price increases, the forced bundling, the slow updates, and the inferior service. There are plenty of consulting groups that can help you renegotiate, and it is generally worth the time and effort to do so. Pushing may not always result in lower costs, but it should result in better products to justify the price.

> *"In banking, pricing is the product."*
>
> *Most pricing systems are designed with one goal in mind: keep lenders from doing bad deals. A successful system, though, should approach it in the exact opposite way: help lenders to do great deals.*

Second, when it comes to technology spending, bankers need to shift from "cost-cutting mode" to "value-adding mode." There is still plenty of growth and revenue to be had in banking, and plenty of opportunity to differentiate. To do that, though, bankers will need to start investing heavily in brain systems and in personnel with the expertise to integrate those systems into the bank's practices and culture. Doing so will build a better customer experience, and bankers know this has always had a lucrative ROI that far outweighs the impact of simply cutting costs.

Banking used to be a cutting edge industry, and it can be again with a slight shift in focus from the heart to the brain.

The Big Four

To get a better understanding of just how powerful and effective a banking ecosystem can be, let's take a closer look at the most important systems, i.e., the Big Four. We'll explain what each system does and how it fits into the overall ecosystem.

Customer Relationship Management

Customer Management — Opportunity Relationship — Priced Opportunity Relationship Profitability — Pricing & Profitability

CRM systems seem to have a fairly nasty reputation in the banking industry. Blame it on the fact that banks are the ideal candidate for CRM, and therefore many tried to adopt those systems when they first became available. Unfortunately, early CRM tools were big, bulky, and expensive, and they didn't really integrate with anything the banks already had in place.

On top of that, early CRMs were incredibly tedious to use. Management teams wrote big checks, and then spent the next several years trying to threaten and bludgeon their employees into actually using them. Management wanted access to data and insights on their sales process, but getting that data required consistent manual input from the staff. The hill simply proved to be too steep in most cases, and the projects were abandoned more often than not. CRM projects started to be viewed as career killers, and many bank executives still carry those battle scars.

However, the tide finally seems to be turning. The CRM technology of today has transformed to be nearly unrecognizable from the earliest versions. These are not your older brother's CRM tools, and the allure of a more efficient and transparent sales process is finally coaxing bankers to take another look. They know that to succeed in today's competitive market, the stack of yellow legal pads in the cabinet can no longer serve as the method for tracking and measuring sales.

Modern CRM systems are usually cloud-based and have become much more than just a way to track sales calls. Many organizations are using them as the foundation for their entire sales, approval, and origination process. Unlike your core system, they have been built from the ground up to handle data coming and going in multiple directions . . . LOTS of data.

A CRM should serve as your central repository for all institutional knowledge about each of your customers. It will tell you who that customer is, what business you do with them, how profitable they are, and what opportunities there are for earning future business.

In addition, CRMs are excellent stage-tracking and task-management tools. They can track the history of all activity with each customer and can be used to schedule future tasks and activities. Think of the CRM as the conveyor belt in your loan assembly line. Once a loan is created on the system, the status can be moved from one process to the next, with an employee completing the necessary work and then handing it off to the next person in line.

Once this is in place, you can actually see the production process in motion. We know bankers who have dashboards that measure sales velocity, how many calls it takes to generate a deal, and how many days it takes at each step in the process. Bottlenecks are found and fixed, and the entire organization gets smarter about selling and servicing their customers.

All of that functionality is why the CRM is not only listed as one of our "Big Four" systems in the brain of the bank, but is at the beginning of the loan origination process. It is where your conversations with customers start, and where you should start your work. Then it can act to keep moving the deal forward until you have met your customer's needs as quickly (and profitably) as possible.

Pricing and Profitability Management

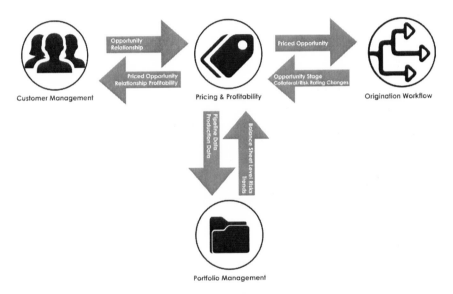

Pricing and profitability management is the easiest one for us; it's the box we fill at PrecisionLender and is the basis for much of this book. As we discussed in Chapter 1, pricing is the most powerful performance lever that a bank has, yet many banks treat it as an afterthought.

We see the full spectrum of solutions in this space, ranging from no solution at all ("The market dictates pricing, so why bother?") to elaborate homemade models. The issue with nearly all of them is that they are entirely disconnected from the rest of the sales process.

The reality in most banks is that pricing is a seat-of-the-pants decision from a lender, based on competitive offers that are determined in a similar fashion. Then, when it's already too late, that deal is plugged into a cumbersome pricing model that is nothing more than a glorified calculator. Even worse, it's a calculator with a binary outcome; the deal either passes the hurdle rate or fails. With this set-up, it is actually impossible for a pricing system to create value. At best, it will cause you to say no to some bad deals that are already well into your process.

The solution, as we discussed in Chapter 4, is to move the pricing decision as close to the customer as you can possibly get it. In terms of systems, that means it should be directly connected to your CRM. This strikes some bankers as an odd pairing. Why would they attach a pricing model to their CRM? Isn't pairing the warm and fuzzy relationship stuff with the cold hard reality of the math a little like mixing oil and water? That might be true in a traditional business, where you are attaching a price to a separate, tangible product. The price for an iPhone, for example, doesn't need much CRM interaction.

In banking, however, pricing is the product. The structure and terms attached to the funds you lend are the solution for your customer, and to get the right fit, you absolutely need all of the context provided by the CRM. In addition, it is the next logical step in the process. Once all of your business development efforts managed in the CRM result in a live opportunity, you will move into formal discussions about the right structure and price for that funding need. For maximum efficiency, lenders should be able to jump directly from their opportunity to a pricing discussion and have the full benefit of knowing the history, relationship status, and profitability of that customer.

All of that context should be combined with a pricing tool that is designed to enable lenders, not block them. Most pricing systems are designed with one goal in mind: keep lenders from doing bad deals. A successful system, though, should approach it in the exact opposite way: help lenders do great deals.

This may seem like a subtle difference, but to the lender, it changes everything. Instead of a pricing model being one more thing that can trip up a deal and keep them from serving their customer, it becomes a sales and negotiation tool that helps them find ways to help their customer. What does this really look like? Most pricing software communicates red lights and warning labels to the lender with these sort of terms:

- The maximum fixed term is 7 years.

- Non-recourse loans are strictly prohibited.

- No loans with LTV >75% will be approved.

● Adding 13 bps to Initial Rate reaches the target
● Adding $8,641 to Initial Fee reaches the target
● Adding 0.58% to Initial Fee reaches the target
● Reducing LTV to 73% reaches the target
● Reducing Maturity to 55 months reaches the target
● Consumer DDA of $126K reaches the opportunity target
● Commercial DDA of $136K reaches the opportunity target
● Consider a Floating or Adjustable Rate to reach target

We have seen huge improvements in performance by altering this approach to using green lights that highlight suggestions (first seven rows in image above) and blue lights that offer more information on the deal (last row in image above). Instead of a list of things to avoid, use a list of options that work. It becomes a menu of solutions that will benefit both the bank and the borrower and helps the lender work through these options with the customer.

Changing the perspective of the tool in turn changes the perspective of the users (which should be the lenders, as they're the ones actually negotiating the deal), enabling them to influence outcomes in a big way. Lenders using this approach win more deals, they win better deals, and they earn loyalty from their customers. Strong relationships aren't built on the golf course; they're built at the negotiating table.

The real magic of integrating pricing and CRM, though, happens after the deal is priced. The pricing of a deal creates a wealth of usable data, as you now have deal terms, scenario details, and profitability results. Those profitability results cover not just the new opportunity but also the profitability of all of the existing business you have with that customer. You now have profitability metrics on individual accounts, bundles of business, and customers that can be rolled up to measure products, lenders, markets, risk grades, collateral types, and dozens of other categories. All of this can be pushed back into the CRM, where it creates context for all future discussions with that customer. And you get it without having to manually enter more data into the CRM.

Banks that have figured this out are the ones taking market share from their competition. They often come into deals with unique offers that cause other banks to scratch their heads and wonder: "How can they possibly offer a deal like that?" The answer isn't that they are simply more aggressive. Their advantage is that they have an insight the competition doesn't, because they have a complete picture of that customer and how winning this next deal impacts their portfolio.

After the deal is priced, it then moves on to the next systems in the value chain: origination workflow management and portfolio management.

Origination Workflow Management

Origination Workflow

Opportunity Stage
Collateral/Risk Rating Changes

Priced Opportunity

Pricing & Profitability

Origination workflow management (we'll call it workflow for short) covers several functions, but the big picture of this phase is that it's where you underwrite and document the transaction. While that sounds simple, the reality is that many of these processes are complicated and messy. This is the first place bankers think of when working on efficiency, as there are sometimes dozens of disparate systems involved that don't communicate with each other. Employees end up keying in the same information multiple times, leading not only to slow turnaround times but also to rampant errors and discrepancies. Banks also end up with data spread across these siloed systems, making it nearly impossible to report on and evaluate risk across systems. Risk grades, collateral, and guarantor data may all be stored in different systems, and none of them link back to the core system.

We see banks taking a couple of approaches to solve this problem. There are a few vendors that have started offering a comprehensive "origination system" or "operating system" for commercial loans, and they have gotten significant traction. The upside is that everything comes in one package and is seamlessly integrated from day one, and the origination process is significantly streamlined. The downside is that, as you can imagine, implementation can be a beast. The system touches everything in the bank and requires an overhaul of just about every process in the loan function.

The second option we see banks taking is to use the CRM as a tracking tool to coordinate all of these systems. Remember, CRM systems do a great job of tracking stages (originally designed for sales stages) and task management. With that functionality, banks are able to create stages, with approval authority, that encompass not only the sale but also the origination.

For example, a stage called "underwriting" can be created, and only certain employees have the ability to move it from "underwriting" to the next stage. When it is marked for underwriting, a series of tasks can be triggered and then assigned, like having an analyst evaluate financial statements and order appraisals. All of the progress is tracked in the CRM system, even if other tools are used to actually complete the work. Then, the results can be stored in a document repository with links in the CRM. It simply acts as a central hub so that anyone involved can see where a deal is in the process, who owns which tasks, and find the documents and data they need.

The key, of course, is that the system has to be used consistently across the organization. This only works if the next step starts off by moving the stages in the CRM system—i.e., it must be properly documented within the CRM system before the next step begins. Analysts can complete their task and then move it to the next stage for official approvals, and then it must be marked as approved to start preparing closing documents.

Whatever the mechanism, though, the workflow systems will need to receive the deal terms from the pricing solution so that they can be underwritten (Is this deal really a grade 3?) and documented (loan agreement matches the economics of the pricing and structure) accurately. This can either be handled as a direct connection to the pricing system, or those deal terms can be pulled from where they are stored in the CRM system. Once all of the workflow processes are completed, and the deal closes, the deal is uploaded to the core system, and from there it will show up in the data feeds to the pricing system to measure its profitability going forward.

Portfolio Management

Last, but not least, are the systems we refer to as portfolio management. In this section, the bank is evaluating all the business that has been booked at an aggregate level. Here, the management team can monitor levels of interest rate and liquidity risk, analyze profit trends, allocate capital, and determine if the tradeoffs for credit risk and return are appropriate. The hard but critical part of this step is linking it back to the tactical business decisions that are made every day, instead of just creating stacks of reports and vanity metrics that don't ever lead to action. This struggle is the reason that portfolio management should be closely connected with pricing. The bank's portfolio metrics should determine the appetite for specific types of deals and risk going forward, and deals can be priced accordingly. Pricing then becomes the steering mechanism by which management can allocate the balance sheet according to high level strategy.

Of course, all of this requires data to serve as a feedback mechanism. How is the pricing translating to production? What types of deals are you winning, and at what profit levels? Where do you have opportunities to achieve growth without relaxing our risk standards?

Data to answer these questions are available in your pricing system. Once you have a grip on how current pricing targets are driving production, you can close the loop by tweaking those targets in the pricing system to get production to align with the goals for the balance sheet.

For example, if you are nearing concentration limits in commercial real estate, you can increase the targets for those and use that limited shelf space for only the best, most profitable, deals. If you have an exposure to rising interest rates, you can adjust targets to win more variable rate deals and core deposits.

Dean's Ecosystem

Dean's vision was impressive, but also daunting. It meant gutting the bank's entire operational platform and rebuilding it. However, a few key philosophies helped guide the way.

First, Dean's team didn't try to do a complete overhaul all at once. They broke the project into manageable pieces, focusing their early efforts on where they would get the biggest impact. There was a "master plan," but it was executed in bite-size chunks.

They decided to start with a pricing system, knowing it would have the biggest revenue impact and thus would help pay for the rest of the overhaul. Following closely behind (and as a part of the selection criteria for the pricing system) was a CRM system that would act as the "conveyor belt" for the entire process.

Second, they chose systems that would "play nice" with all of the surrounding systems. This meant looking at options outside the list of typical bank vendors, who tend to build closed systems and charge dearly for clunky integrations. Dean chose vendors that embraced application program interfaces (APIs), software that makes connecting all the systems much simpler and more efficient.

Third, Dean's team added resources and capabilities so that if something wasn't available out of the box, they could build it in house. Yes, that meant writing some code, but it wasn't code to build complex and hard-to-maintain proprietary systems; it was code to connect and automate various parts of the ecosystem. Having already selected the right vendors and systems, Dean's coders were often just connecting already available end points or requesting that new end points be surfaced by the vendors.

In less than two years, Dean's bank had overhauled the process from end to end. It took a lot of time and resources, but they now have an infrastructure in place that is tangibly different from the competition, not just in terms of efficiency—though it certainly is more efficient—but in terms of customer experience.

Their commercial customers now get fast, personal, and customized responses from the bank, and employees don't have to spend their time and energy focused on internal procedures and policies. Instead, they have very customer-focused conversations that help them best match the bank's products to the customer's needs.

The results speak for themselves; Dean's bank has generated organic growth of nearly 40% per year since putting the ecosystem in place, and has done so with higher levels of profit and less risk than they had while the portfolio was stagnant. The ROI on the ecosystem is breathtaking, and they are able to use those profits to continue evolving and refining the system.

CHAPTER 9: CHOOSING THE RIGHT TOOL

> Screw up a big technology purchase and you'll be connected with that failure as long as you're at the bank . . . which may not be much longer.

Of course, if that were simple to do what Greg's bank did in Chapter 8, we'd see a lot more pricing ecosystems out there. Instead, what we often find are a bunch of cautionary tales about what can go wrong when you're trying to add new systems and solutions at a bank.

So how do you avoid becoming one of those stories? How do you figure out what to buy and which vendor to buy it from?

How NOT to Buy Technology at a Bank

(The following is Dallas's story of an ill-fated trip to the grocery story. But trust us, this could just easily have been Jim or Carl, or maybe even you.)

Have you ever turned a simple shopping trip into a complete and utter failure? A few weeks ago, my wife made out a detailed grocery list for me, including specific brands and how much of each item to purchase. It looked idiot-proof. But looks can be deceiving.

I spent the next 90 minutes driving around town like a mad man, visiting three different stores to get everything on the list. I returned home triumphant, ready to be praised for my grit and determination. I had only forgotten one thing (milk), which is way better than my typical trip. My wife, though, was not nearly as proud of me as I expected.

"What is all of this stuff? And where is the milk?"

You see, it turns out that when I got to the store, I grabbed the wrong list from the passenger seat of my truck. It happened to be the list from a few days before, and I never noticed. The correct list only had four items, and the milk had a star beside it, because it was the one thing we REALLY needed to make dinner. Oops.

In this case, my shopping mistake wasn't too disastrous. Sure, we had no milk and doubles of everything else, but in the grand scheme of things, we will survive.

Five Technology Shopping Mistakes to Avoid

What about banks, though? Is it possible for them to be as bad at shopping as Dallas is? When it comes to technology, the answer is a resounding YES.

The issue, though, is that mistakes in technology shopping don't just leave banks stuck with expensive, inefficient systems. Those subpar systems also provide a lousy experience for their customers. This is especially true now, as banks around the world are busy spending unprecedented amounts to overhaul their technology stacks[11]. These shopping blunders can cripple an organization for years.

Dallas has spent years as a banker sitting through meetings with vendors, and a few more sitting on the other side of the table. He's seen plenty of examples of technology purchase decisions gone awry. The memory of sitting in a board room around 10 years ago trying to explain to his

---

[11] Lodge, Gareth, Hua Zhang, and Jacob Jegher. "IT Spending in Banking: A Global Perspective." IT Spending in Banking: A Global Perspective | Celent. N.p., 5 Feb. 2015. Web. 17 Feb. 2017. <http://celent.com/reports/it-spending-banking-global-perspective-2>.

directors how a virtual server worked is still fresh in his mind. Let's just say that they weren't thrilled with the idea of spending thousands of dollars to have their bank run on "imaginary hardware."

While a lack of technical knowledge is certainly a hindrance, these five recurring issues are the ones that cause real damage. If you are sitting in a meeting and hear one of these lines, some red flags should immediately be raised.

1: Either IT or a procurement team makes every buying decision.

"Is this software? Then IT has to decide."

Your IT and procurement staff should absolutely be a part of every purchasing decision. But remember what their goals typically look like. Their jobs are to A) make sure new systems don't break anything or expose the bank to undue risk and B) save money.

Both are necessary, but both are actually due diligence items that should be addressed after the business lines have found a tool that meets their needs. If the IT or procurement groups are running the show, the process is generally slow and tedious, as the team searches for reasons not to buy.

The best banks let the business lines run the process and make final buying decisions, subject to verification that the new systems don't break anything. When prospects are struggling with this while evaluating our pricing platform, we suggest the approach used by one of our best clients.

He gathered his top commercial lenders in a room for a demo and told them, "I'll be back in an hour. Tell me if this is something that you would actually use and would help you do your job." In an hour he not only had his answer, but also early support from the people who would be the system's end users.

2: Decisions get derailed by "turf defenders."

"Why do we even need this? My Excel model does the same thing, just without the bells and whistles."

There is a saying in the sales world that you are always competing against an established competitor. This is especially true in banking, where there is typically a budget built around what's already in place and little room to add new categories of systems. So when a new system is added into the budget, someone else is getting something taken away, even if that new system deals with an area that the incumbent systems don't address.

The problem arises when people start defending their turf by putting their self-interest ahead of the bank's interests. This is basic human nature, but some banks allow this to have an out-sized influence on the decision. The results can be ugly. These banks are now not only working with inferior legacy technology (or homemade solutions), but they also have allowed little fiefdoms to crop up in which individuals are using their specialized knowledge to protect themselves or elevate their own status.

3: Resources are not allocated by the ROI of the project.

"We agree that this is a *must have* and could make us a lot of money. But, we have so many other things going on, we just can't do it yet. Check back later."

Would you like to venture a guess on how many actually implement it "later" at that check-in? There are always a bunch of projects going on and new things being implemented. Celent's 2015 study on bank technology spending, "IT Spending in Banking: A Global Perspective" (cited on pg. 116), found that more than half of banks' total budgets were being spent on security, compliance, and core systems. Should you really delay something that is accretive to earnings or customer experience because you are too busy with a multi-year roll-out of a back-office system?

4: The process is owned by a committee instead of an individual.

"We will discuss internally, and then someone will get back to you."

Like most things involving a committee, if everyone owns it, then really no one owns it. The best banks insist on naming individual owners of every project. Someone's name is attached to every decision, adding both responsibility and accountability.

One champion pushing for a decision will get to an answer much faster. A quick "yes" means that the project stays on track, but sometimes a quick "no" is just as valuable. It saves an entire team of people countless hours of sitting through demos, follow-up calls, and check-ins from salespeople that ultimately aren't heading anywhere useful.

5: There is no defined process or timeline.

"I'm not sure what the next steps are. I think we have a few others who need to see it, so let's set up another demo and we'll go from there."

This is probably the most marked difference in the banks that excel at purchasing versus those that don't. The best banks know exactly how they go about making these decisions. They have a clearly defined process, including precise steps, expected timeframes, and clear designations of who is responsible for making final decisions.

The process at most banks is much fuzzier; no one is sure who has the official authority to decide, and so no decision is ever made. Plus, any decision that does

> *"The best banks choose the best tools and quickly get them up and running. Those tools then help add revenue or improve efficiency, leaving the bank with more resources to invest in even more tools. Wash, rinse, repeat, and pretty soon they have left their competitors in the dust."*

get made is then thrown into a chaotic budgeting process where it may or may not actually get funding.

Quick to Decide, Quick to Revenue

While the symptoms and causes may vary, nearly all of these issues result in wasted time. The best banks move through the decision process as quickly as possible so they can focus their time on actually implementing tools instead of evaluating them indefinitely.

Once the process is in place, it becomes a powerful feedback loop. The best banks choose the best tools and quickly get them up and running. Those tools then help add revenue or improve efficiency, leaving the bank with more resources to invest in even more tools. Wash, rinse, repeat, and pretty soon they have left their competitors in the dust.

The banks that struggle with this, however, end up with the bank equivalent of no milk and doubles of everything else: old, expensive systems and no ability to differentiate themselves.

The Five C's of Bank Vendor Assessment and Selection

If you've avoided the pitfalls listed above, congratulations! But you're not out of the woods yet. Having the right framework in place for technology purchasing is just step one. Step two is figuring out which vendor you're going to do business with.

This is a daunting task. As Carl puts it, in any given week we'll likely do more product demos and presentations than you and your management team will participate in over the course of an entire year. That's true for most of the vendors out there selling tech to banks.

All those repetitions mean that vendors are pretty good at looking good. So it's very likely that at the end of each vendor presentation you sit through, you'll have a very favorable view of what you have just seen.

How then do you separate the promise from the reality? What sort of questions could you ask each vendor that could be used to underwrite the promise of the demo?

Vendor Underwriting

The great news for banks is that you already have a trusted framework for doing this. In fact, this capability is at the heart of one of the most important things that you do every day: credit underwriting.

It's a disciplined process of asking questions and gathering information to underwrite a borrower's promise to repay a loan (plus a promised return). Most credit underwriting is based around a useful framework known as The Five C's of Credit: Character, Capacity, Capital, Collateral, and Conditions.

Vendor Assessment & Selection

C→C→C→C→C

| Company | Culture | Customers | Churn | Conditions |

We looked back over the thousands of demos we've done over the years as a vendor to banks. We identified the best questions we were asked by potential clients, either during the demo or later as part of their vendor due-diligence process. Two very interesting patterns emerged when we examined these questions and the clients who asked them.

The prospective clients who consistently asked the best questions took a credit underwriter's approach to vendor and solution assessment and vendor due diligence. They were trying to underwrite the promise of the demo with facts and evidence. The questions they asked could be grouped into what we now refer to as the Five C's of Vendor Assessment and Selection: Company, Culture, Customers, Churn, and Conditions.

It's no coincidence that these Five C's map over, almost directly, to the Five C's of Credit. Those who apply the credit discipline to their vendor selection process don't view the vendor's solution as merely an expense. Instead, they view it as an asset (like a loan) that requires an initial investment of both time and capital but should, if the promises are met, pay back their investment and provide a meaningful return with minimal risk. Their goal is to underwrite that risk.

Here's a brief description of each of the Five C's of Vendor Assessment and Selection, including some of the best questions in each category that we've been asked by prospects. We've also included some advice on how to frame your questions and how to interpret the answers you get from the vendors. (A more comprehensive list of questions will be included in the Appendix.)

Company and Culture

Is the vendor someone you can trust; someone you'd be proud to do business with? It's not an easy judgment to make. The questions you ask here need to reveal enough facts and evidence to enable you to reach a confident conclusion.

There is an old saying in credit underwriting: "A '1 Credit' is Bill Gates married to Mother Teresa with joint accounts." In other words, it's a borrower with both the proven ability to repay and the moral character to actually do so. You can think about Company and Culture in a very similar way. Understanding the company (its size, financial strength, ability to attract and retain great people) will help you underwrite their ability to deliver. Understanding their culture (how they measure customer success, how they handle difficult situations, how transparent, open and honest they are with their customers and prospects) will help you understand whether they will actually deliver on their promises.

Questions and Answers

Ask about the size of the company and, in particular, the size of the group that supports, maintains, and develops the product you're considering. And does that group work with other products, or just this one?

The vendors' responses to these questions will reveal a great deal. Do they answer in terms that are more relevant to you or more relevant to them? Or in ways that seem to obfuscate rather than clarify?

Do they talk about number of employees, or about amount of revenue or market capitalization (terms relevant to them)? Or do they describe the actual size of the group dedicated to developing and supporting the product they're asking you to buy (terms relevant to you)?

When assessing the company and its ability to deliver, you want to understand how much the company is actually investing in the product, in its development, and its support. Is this investment declining or accelerating? The number of issues you'll encounter and how quickly and completely they'll be resolved is a direct consequence of the level of dedicated investment to the product. The fact that they have 5,000 employees serving other clients using other products is, at best, irrelevant and, at worst, a deliberate distraction or overstatement.

The culture questions are ways to essentially find out how the vendor determines whether their clients are getting a return on their investment, what the vendor does if clients aren't getting this return, and whether the vendor even cares about this. The answers that a vendor gives here, just like in credit underwriting, will have an enormous impact on how you view the "Conditions" of this relationship (the fifth and final C). There are two big things to look for in their answers to the culture questions.

First, if you ask how they measure customer success, they may try to answer this with customer satisfaction survey results. Customer satisfaction is necessary in ensuring customer success, but it's not the be-all end-all, either. Pay close attention to the vendor's answers here and see if they align with their customer retention answers in the *Churn* section below.

High customer satisfaction with low customer retention indicates that their satisfaction surveys are doing a poor job of measuring success.

Second, every vendor should be able to tell a story (or two) about an unsuccessful customer. No vendor is perfect; there will always be a few cases where it just did not work out. Through these stories you should get a sense of the vendor's level of openness and honesty. Do they blame the customer? Do they blame external factors, such as the economy? Or do they focus on what they could have done better either in the sales process or in the delivery process? Most importantly, what did they do about it? Did they make things right?

Customers

Every solution requires an investment of both time and money on your part. In exchange, vendors offer the promise of a return on that investment. There are really only three meaningful ways this return can be delivered:

- Increased Revenue through:
    - Volume improvement (sell more)
    - Pricing improvement (charge more)
- Decreased Expense through:
    - Increased efficiency (do more with less)
    - Elimination of expenses/loss (just need less)
- Decreased Risk through:
    - Reduced likelihood of losing revenue
    - Reduced likelihood of increasing expenses

Any vendor should be able to connect their solution's value proposition to one or more of these. If this is not crystal clear very early in the process, move on. In banking terms, there's no need to underwrite a loan to someone who can't demonstrate a clear path to even repaying the principal.

Growth and retention (see *Churn* below) of customers are very strong evidence of a positive ROI. If these numbers are flat or declining, you should be concerned. A growing customer base almost always leads to growing investment in the product and its associated support and service. A declining customer base often leads to just the opposite. If the vendor has described a growing level of investment in the product, yet you see a declining customer base, you know eventually something has to give.

Questions and Answers

Simply asking the vendor how many customers they have can be revealing. If they say they have 10,000 customers and it quickly becomes apparent with the next question that only 50 are relevant to the current product they're selling to you, it's a red flag and should get you thinking about other claims they may be overstating.

You want to narrow the discussion down to the set of customers that is most relevant to your situation so you can determine if future investment in this product will be aligned with your needs. What segment of the vendor's customer base is growing? This is where investments in the product and service will be focused going forward. Figure out what that means for you . . . it could be good or bad, depending on how you compare to those current customers. Do they have customers that are similar to you? If so, ask for names so you can speak with them.

Churn

Churn is the single best metric for underwriting the value proposition of the vendor.

It correlates, more than anything else, with actual customer success. Jeffery Gitomer said it clearly in the title of his book: *Customer Satisfaction Is Worthless, Customer Loyalty Is Priceless*. Customers only keep paying for things that are producing benefits that exceed their costs.

Think of it this way. For a company that charges $10,000/year for a service, with annual renewals, each year the company essentially conducts a survey of its customers. This survey has only one question: Did the value you received from using this product greatly exceed the investment of both time and money required to use it?

If you answer "yes" to this question, you staple a check for $10,000 to your response. If you answer "no," it costs you nothing. By definition, this survey has a 100% response rate. The percentage of "no" responses is commonly known as "churn."

Buying any subscription-based software as a service (SaaS) solution and not asking the vendor about churn would be like booking a loan without asking to see financials. Yet banks do it all the time. You should ask for the results of this survey above all others.

Questions and Answers

You can look at vendor's churn rate in two ways: the percentage of clients who renew each year, or the percentage of contract revenue that's renewed (net revenue renewal rate). The first metric will show you whether the vendor is losing clients. The second metric takes into account whether the vendor is being forced to cut price to keep business or, conversely, if customers are expanding their business and buying more stuff. The latter could lead to a Net Revenue Renewal Rate greater than 100% . . . a great sign.

Unfortunately, as with all metrics, churn rate has some blind spots. It will miss customers who left in the middle of their contract because they were not up for renewal. Be sure to ask about this, especially if the vendor pushes for multi-year commitments. (More on this in the *Conditions* section below.)

Ask the vendor about their strongest competitors and how they compete with them. This is where the best vendors separate themselves. If there are four competitive vendors for a particular product, odds are you'll only get a straight and honest answer to this question from one of them. That vendor will be the market leader, with the lowest churn.

The market leader competes by offering results and references based on actual customer success. Others may compete by offering significantly lower prices and push for longer terms. It's not at all unusual for the market leader to have 100 clients switch from a lower-priced competitor for every one client they have churn away to another vendor.

Conditions

Just as in credit underwriting, you must also understand and evaluate the conditions of the deal in the context of what you've learned from the other four C's. These conditions serve to either mitigate or exacerbate the risk.

Questions and Answers

Generally, you'll get the actual terms in a written proposal and later a full contract, but it's still worth asking now about how they price, whether they offer guarantees, the typical contract term, etc. Take good notes; you'll want to ensure the actual contract reflects the answers you were given.

With vendor assessments, the linkage between the conditions and the other four C's is even more pronounced because, unlike in credit underwriting, the vendor is setting the proposed terms and conditions. If you've done a good job in assessing the Company, Culture, Customers, and Churn of this vendor, there should be no surprises from the Conditions.

Consider the case where a vendor's new customer growth is slowing and, at the same time, they're losing customers to competitive solutions. When they offer you a rock-bottom price in exchange for a five-year commitment, is it really any mystery as to why? They're insuring the risk that you'll cancel on them, and they know better than anyone what that's worth. Buyer beware.

Putting the Pieces Together

The trend toward buying powerful, highly specialized solutions (particularly cloud-based software solutions) will likely continue as more banks look to improve performance, increase efficiency, and reduce cost.

The stakes are high for banks to get it right. That means identifying the vendors you can truly rely on. Fortunately, you've already developed a framework for understanding which borrowers are most likely to give you an acceptable return on your investment. There's no reason you shouldn't know the same thing about your vendors.

What to Look for in a Pricing Tool

Doing all that due diligence won't matter if the vendor doesn't have the product that fits your needs.

As you might guess by everything we have covered in earlier chapters, we have found that a pricing tool needs to be much more than just a calculator. From way back in Chapter 2, where we introduced the Price Setting and Price Getting concepts, we know that getting the math right is necessary, but it is not sufficient in itself. Your bank must have a way of actually executing on the price, and getting it on the books at the needed volumes for your business to grow and prosper. To that end, a pricing solution will be as much a sales and negotiation tool as it is a calculator of returns, and that means that there are two vital characteristics that need to be present.

Start at the Customer, End at the Bank

First, the solution must start at the lender's interaction with their borrower and then work backward. If the entire system is designed from the bank's perspective, you have already lost. A customer doesn't care about a facility risk grade, or overhead cost, or how much economic capital is being allocated. These are necessary for the bank to get to a price, but if this is the sole focus of your tool, it is also going to become the primary focus of your lenders.

Instead, the tool should facilitate a better conversation with borrowers. The terms used in the solution should not be internal bank jargon, but should be deal terms as they would be discussed with a borrower. You talk to borrowers about collateral and guarantees, not facility grades. You talk about the length of the project, not the maximum terms the bank allows. You offer options based on what the borrower is willing and able to do, not based on what the bank's standard cookie-cutter structures look like.

All of this, of course, requires the system to be intuitive and incredibly easy for lenders to use. We've stressed the importance of giving your lenders the ability to make decisions in the moment, while the borrower is sitting across the table from them. You can't do that if you're constantly hunting around the screen, looking for relevant information.

Want an idea of what it looks like when a lot of important data is presented in a way that's easy for the user to digest and act upon? Look no further than your fantasy football site. Every day during the season, fantasy football players (present company included) log into million-dollar websites that manage their drafts, provide in-depth analysis, graph recent trends for dozens of metrics, and even provide meaningful statistical projections.

"For the tool to work effectively as a sales enabler, you should think in terms of the profit levels you are aiming at, not the bare minimum you will accept. This allows lenders to see the returns the bank desires, but also to make exceptions where it makes good business sense to do so, like with the bank's very best relationships."

Even novice players can use the clean, simple interface and the wealth of data to play what was once an overly complex game. Not sure if you should make a trade? The site will show you projections for each potential lineup for the rest of the season, allowing you to quickly evaluate the pros and cons of the deal.

How does this compare to your pricing tool? We're guessing that for most of you, these two aren't even in the same universe. If your lenders have far superior software for playing a free fantasy football game than they have for managing multi-million dollar loan deals, then you can understand why they are frustrated. It must be a priority to provide them with the proper tools to effectively do their jobs, and that means a pricing tool that is actually valuable to them. It should help them, in real time, have better conversations with their borrowers that enable better deal making instead of being an overly complex calculator that is used a week after the deal has already been negotiated.

Connect the Front of the Bank with the Back

The second vital characteristic of a successful pricing tool is that it must be the conduit for communication between the back of the bank (the Price Setters) and the front of the bank (the Price Getters). As we covered in Chapter 7, transparency is one of the key ingredients to effective pricing and relationship building in a bank. One of the reasons that so many banks struggle with transparency, however, is that the logistics are really hard.

How you do let all of the lenders in your entire footprint know what the bank's strategy looks like? In turn, how do they let us know what the competition in the marketplace is doing? Because pricing is the fulcrum between the front and back of the bank, the pricing tool MUST act as the means of communication. It is the means by which management can adjust profitability targets to steer the balance sheet, pricing aggressively the types of business that best fit the bank's strategy and increasing prices on the types of business for which the bank has little appetite. It is also the means by which management can see the results of those targets. Is volume shrinking because targets are too high? Are you seeing too many deals priced below the targets as exceptions? Or did you see a big jump in volume, and could you possibly be leaving money on the table because we are too far below market?

Logistically this is all communicated through profitability targets and results (both of which are, of course, adjusted for risk). Notice we say targets and not hurdle rates. For the tool to work effectively as a sales enabler, you should think in terms of the profit levels you are aiming at, not the bare minimum you will accept (which should be one of the few closely guarded secrets in a transparent organization). This allows lenders to see the returns the bank desires, but also to make exceptions where it makes good business sense to do so, like with the bank's very best relationships.

Using targets instead of predefined structures with hurdle rates also allows the lenders to see a variety of options on how to reach those targeted returns. It shouldn't always be about rate, or else you risk becoming used car salesmen haggling back and forth over the one flexible part of the deal. Instead, all of the levers should be available, including term, rate type, collateral, amortization schedule, and expanding the opportunity to include additional business.

While these two vital characteristics were described in terms of the pricing tool, they should also be applied to the other pieces of the ecosystem outlined in Chapter 8. The CRM tools, workflow tools, and portfolio analysis tools should all stay true to the same concepts. They must focus on the end users, and they must facilitate better communication between the front and back of the bank (and therefore between the bank and its customers). With the right vendors and the right tools chosen, you are well on your way to arming your bankers with everything they need to build the meaningful, long-lasting relationships that will define your brand.

Building a Partnership with Your Vendors

Purchasing technology at your bank isn't merely a transaction. It's the start of a long- term relationship with your vendor. Cornerstone Advisors, the authors of the insightful and entertaining Gonzo Banker blog, have a post titled "Is Your Vendor a Partner?"[12] It lists 10 questions you should ask yourself to determine if your vendor behaves more like a partner and less like a salesman. We won't go into all 10, but here are some of the most important points they made:

Your vendor should do research for you, not vice versa.

During their sales pitch, all vendors portray themselves as experts in their fields. It's a point they have to prove, otherwise why would you buy from them? If you've got the right vendor, they don't stop sharing their expertise once you've made your purchase. Instead, they keep sending you newsletters, sharing webinars, inviting you to conferences, etc. If you're at the point where sometimes you're a little exasperated by the amount of times your vendor reaches out to you in a month, then you're in a good partnership. It's okay if they overshare. It's not okay if they ignore.

Your vendor needs to be able to play nice with other vendors.

There is no overarching single solution to everything a bank needs done. That means your vendor's tool needs to be able to interact with the tools of other vendors. If your vendor has developed a variety of integrations and is constantly working on adding more, then you're well positioned to be able to expand your technology stack. If not, then you're in for a lot of work on your end and a whole lot of headaches.

Your account representative needs to be your advocate.

When you're struggling with a problem, you shouldn't be the one updating your account representative on what's going on. They should be the ones bringing the issue to the attention of the right people and making sure it stays front and center until it is either resolved or there's at least an

---

[12] Roche, Terence. "Is Your Vendor a Partner? Ask These 10 Questions to Find Out." Gonzobanker.com. N.p., 09 Sept. 2016. Web. 17 Feb. 2017. <http://www.gonzobanker.com/2016/09/is-your-vendor-a-partner/>.

explanation why it won't be. It's a lot harder to ignore the squeaky wheel when it's squeaking from across the office instead of across a phone line.

Your vendor should work to make you a better customer.

This goes back to the churn questions you should be asking during vendor underwriting. Follow the logic here: Vendors have low churn if their customers are happy. Customers are happy when they're having success with the tool they're using. Therefore, smart vendors take steps to ensure their customers know how to get the most out of their tool.

Not-so-smart vendors take a passive approach, assuming everything is fine unless they hear otherwise from the customer. Sometimes that's fine; you might be doing well on your own. A vendor that is unwilling to commit resources to ensure your success, however, is not the type of vendor you're going to want to lean on when you do hit a snag.

Granted, having a vendor stick their nose into your business and point out ways you could be doing your job better can be a little awkward, even a little annoying at times. As Gonzo Banker points out, however: "Partners don't shy away from uncomfortable conversations."

Conclusion

If you're a little apprehensive about buying technology at your bank, that's completely understandable. There's a great deal at stake. Get it right, and your star will rise right alongside the bank's. Get it wrong, and you'll be connected with that failure as long as you're at the bank . . . which may not be much longer.

Doing nothing might seem safe, but remember, it's still a choice. You will have made a choice to stand pat and hope that all the trends leading to shrinking margins and fewer banks will somehow magically reverse themselves. Good luck with that.

Technology buying is important, but don't worry. Just take a deep breath and think of this decision in familiar terms: risk and return.

If you know the major pitfalls to avoid and the right questions to ask potential vendors, you've decreased your purchase risk considerably. Then, if you have the right goals in mind when buying the technology and you've formed a strong relationship with the right vendor, you've increased your potential return as well.

Take those steps and you'll get the buy-in you need from the key players at the bank. But your work isn't done there. Next you'll need buy-in from the actual users.

CHAPTER 10: GET YOUR LENDERS TO ENGAGE, NOT REVOLT

> Design everything to start at the lender and work backward. If the end users don't use it, nothing else matters.

Our Story So Far

If you've made it this far, you've embraced the concept of a pricing ecosystem, and you've got an idea of what pricing tool you're going to buy and how you're going to make that purchasing decision.

Now comes the really fun part: Getting your lenders to actually use it.

Before you can get to that point though, rolling out a new pricing system requires some work on a broader, higher level at the bank. It's a necessity given the cross-functional and complex nature of pricing. Embracing the Price Getting aspect—and everything that follows from that—requires deep organizational change. You need to put a great deal of thought into the cultural and planning phases of implementation.

Embracing Change

Banks get a bad rap when it comes to change. Almost every piece we read on bank innovation mentions that amazing new technology is available, it's just that the darn banks are no good at implementing new things. Admittedly, we've said similar things on our blog and podcast.

To be fair, though, banks actually have done a pretty good job with innovating over the last decade or so, particularly given all the other pressing issues they've had to handle. How many of those smug fintech competitors have had to rebuild nearly every process in their shop to comply with thousands of pages' worth of new regulations?

Struggling with change is not unique to banking, as all organizations in all lines of business face similar issues. The simple fact is that humans are creatures of habit. We see this firsthand when we roll out our pricing platform in new banks.

The technology part of it is incredibly easy. As we are a cloud-based solution, it is simply a matter of turning on their account and then showing them how to configure it. The real pain comes when we take away the tools the bank had previously been using and try to build new processes around our solution. The habits are WAY harder to change than the tools.

Over the last several years, we have rolled out the PrecisionLender pricing and profitability solution to hundreds of banks and thousands of users. To be frank, we've achieved varying levels of success during implementation.

A few clients took to the new approach quickly, and they were up and running with huge results right out of the gate. A few others haven't been as successful, and they have struggled to get the right people on board with all of the changes. Most fall somewhere in between. They see tangible results in a short time but know they are

"Struggling with change is not unique to banking, as all organizations in all lines of business face similar issues."

The simple fact is that humans are creatures of habit.

still leaving money on the table through their inability to get everyone rowing in the same direction.

In short, we know firsthand that change is really hard, especially when you are changing something like pricing, which is so cross-functional and touches almost every part of the bank. While we've earned our implementation stripes rolling out software in banks, the lessons we've learned there can be applied to change (of tools, processes, people, etc.) in any type of organization.

To understand why the habits are so much harder to change than the technology, we'll share a popular story that just happens to be based on some bad science. Stay with us and we'll explain the bad science part.

The Five Chimps Experiment

Years ago, scientists did a study with chimpanzees. They put five chimps in a small room that had a ladder at the center with bananas at the top. Whenever one of the chimps would climb the ladder to get the bananas, the scientists would spray the other four chimps with a hose. Chimps are smart, so it didn't take long for them to figure this out. Pretty soon, whenever a chimp would get hungry and decide to try for the bananas, the others would pull him away. If he was persistent, he would get a beating from his fellow chimps. No one likes to get sprayed with a hose.

Then came the really interesting part of the study. The scientists removed one of the five chimps, and replaced it with a new one. Of course, the new chimp immediately tried to climb the ladder, and received a beating for it. He eventually caught on, and gave up on the bananas.

The scientists then removed another of the original chimps, and replaced him with another newbie. Just as expected, he started to climb the ladder and received a beating from all the others. Then came the surprising part: The first newbie joined in on the beating of the second one, even though Newbie No. 1 had never been sprayed with a hose. He didn't know why it was a bad thing that Newbie No. 2 was trying to climb the ladder, but he helped pound on Newbie No. 2 nonetheless.

The scientists kept replacing chimps one by one, and pretty soon they had five chimps in the room that had never been sprayed with a hose. And yet, any time one of the chimps would start to climb the ladder, the other four would administer a beating. They had no idea why they were doing this, just that it had always been this way.

Sound familiar?

Now the bad science part: It turns out there's no evidence this experiment ever happened. Instead, it seems that people have blended stories about a couple of studies, and the chimps with the ladder exhibit behaviors that are really only shown in studies of humans. The mythical five chimps experiment gained widespread popularity nonetheless, because it struck a chord with nearly everyone. We have all been in situations where a behavior or practice is deeply embedded in the organization, and getting rid of it is nearly impossible. No one knows why they are doing it, just that it has always been that way.

Where Can You Make Mistakes?

Being aware of this phenomenon, though, doesn't solve the problem. After years of implementing new systems and processes in hundreds of banks for thousands of employees, we have learned a few key principles.

We'll start with the foundation of change, which is all about culture. Of course, the overall culture won't change overnight. Instead, we will touch on one small but important aspect: Is it okay to make mistakes in your bank?

In a lot of banks, mistakes of any kind are simply not tolerated. It's understandable. As Dallas's first boss told him when he got into banking, "If the owner of a retail store is right 95% of the time, he becomes Sam Walton. If a banker is right 95% of the time, he is out of a job." When it comes to credit, regulatory compliance, or fraud, that is absolutely correct. The problems occur when you allow that mentality to pervade across the organization and creep into all of your decision making.

If you think about this from the perspective of your staff, you will understand why your new initiatives meet so much resistance. The status quo is proven and safe. If you stick to that, no disaster can befall you, and if something bad does happen, it's not your fault. You were just following the established procedures and the entrenched tools. Trying something new, though, is risky. What if you change a process and it fails? Now you can be blamed for rocking the boat when you should have just stuck with what was working.

To overcome this, the leadership of the bank needs to differentiate the areas where perfection is the standard (credit, etc.) from the areas where it is okay try new things and fail. For example, what if you tried having the lenders use the pricing tool instead of having the analysts do it for them? Granted, they might enter it wrong. On the other hand, it might speed up the process and also might allow that lender to come up with a better, more profitable structure that the borrower prefers. Unless everyone knows that it's okay to try something like this, however, you will get big push back on every small change and you'll miss out on a lot of potential benefits.

"The end users, those who will be most affected, should not be the last to know."

Getting their early buy-in and giving them a seat at the table will head off a ton of problems later on.

The key is to match up the risk and reward for your employees. In the right areas, make sure they know it's okay to try to climb the ladder. Make sure they know there is the potential for a reward, and—more importantly—that there is no hose or beating for them and their teammates if they fail.

Going from Concept to Reality

Getting your bank on board with the concept of change is one thing. Turning that concept into reality, in the form of a project that fundamentally alters the way the bank does its business, is another thing entirely.

Here are a few tips on how to take those ideas out of the clouds and into your bank's everyday operations.

Sell the Future State

Once the foundation has been set with a culture that embraces change, it's time to start selling. For any big project to succeed, you have to sell the future state and all its accompanying glory. Everyone knows the journey may be a difficult one, but if they can at least see the light at the end of the tunnel, they can get on board with it.

There are two important distinctions to make here.

First, the benefit of this future state is all in the eye of the beholder. For example, when we look at who our change champion is at each of our clients, we see an almost equal split between finance and lending.

In the finance/treasury world, they may be excited about better risk-adjusted returns, improved margins, and better allocation of capital. The lenders? Not so much. They need to know how it will affect their ability to serve their customers and grow their portfolios. If the project creates an impediment to either of those, then it is likely doomed from the outset, regardless of what it can do for margins and capital allocation.

In a similar vein, if the lenders are excited about getting a sales and negotiation tool to win more deals, the finance group may have a little heartburn: Are they letting the foxes guard the henhouse?

An effective project will take an inventory of the needs and concerns for each stakeholder and make sure there is a future state for all of them that is worth the effort. If you don't have that, then you might need to re-think the whole project.

Second, selling the future state doesn't mean you need an unalterable master plan. You will learn as you go, and plans will most definitely change. You aren't selling a precise road map, but rather the improvements that will be seen once you get there.

Get User Input Early and Often

In the "old days" of software and systems (i.e., 5–10 years ago), all vendors knew to sell directly to the C-suite, and then the bosses would impose the tool on the end users. It was used because it was required, but the end users often hated it, as it was chosen by people who would have the least amount of interaction with it.

A classic example is the early versions of CRM systems, where management teams wanted all of the data and insights into the sales process, but they were not the ones who had to actually do all of that manual data entry. Instead, the software was just something inflicted on the staff so the bosses could get the reports they were after. Let's just say the results weren't what was promised, and a lot of organizations soon abandoned some very expensive projects.

We see a similar issue with pricing. If the end users—in our case the lenders—don't use it, then nothing else matters. It doesn't matter how robust our reporting is or how flexible the product configurations are if the lenders hate it. Therefore, we design everything to start at the lender and work backward. In our opinion, this extends all the way to the buying and implementation process.

Before buying PrecisionLender, we insist that the lenders see it and agree that it's a platform that will be valuable to them. We also suggest putting a couple top producers on the project team. They usually resist at first, but it is the best way to make sure they get a voice in the process. We don't want to impose a platform on them; we want to let them help design something that allows them to do their job better.

This principle applies to any new tool or process. The end users, those who will be most affected, should not be the last to know. Getting their early buy-in and giving them a seat at the table will head off a ton of problems later on. After all, it's a little harder to revolt against a tool or process when you had a vote at the very beginning. Skin in the game is a powerful motivator to make it work.

Clear Ownership

This is a topic we have discussed many times, but every new endeavor needs a clear owner. Someone needs to have both the responsibility and the authority to move the project along, and with that comes clear accountability. Committees can certainly be used to help, but there must be an individual's name attached to it if you want it to be done on time and on budget. In our world we refer to this person as a Chief Pricing Officer, but every project needs a similar role.

As one of Dallas's bosses once told him, "There are lots of people involved, but I'm putting you in charge so I have one throat to choke." Dallas definitely got the point, and made sure that the project was herded through as planned.

Conversely, if your bank chooses not to implement change, someone needs to own that decision as well. When the outcome of staying status quo rests on someone's shoulders, it no longer becomes a state that's easily defaulted to in lieu of change.

Bite-Size Pieces

The most common objection we get from prospects is that because they already have so much on their plate, they can't imagine adding another project . . . especially one that will touch so many parts of their business. This sentiment doesn't change just because the bosses decide it's a priority. The project team often walks into the kickoff meeting expecting the worst, as their plates are full of other projects that are behind schedule and are falling short of promised results.

To combat this, when implementing PrecisionLender we break the process down into manageable pieces. Every step from configuration to user training is reduced to a bite-size chunk, and then assigned to a person with a due date. Once we start making progress, we communicate that over and over again.

When a team can see measurable forward progress after a couple of weeks, and realize that it actually wasn't so painful, the project tends to pick up momentum. Yes, this takes a fair amount of advance planning, but it's always worth it.

Shorten the Time-to-Value

The final item on our list is one that is closely related to several others, but it's important enough to merit its own section. We see a lot of banks that do a great job with selling the future state but still wind up in projects that eventually become so long and drawn out they lose momentum and stall before completion. Banks are usually beholden to the annual budget cycle, which means anything that stretches out too far without generating results runs the risk of losing resources.

To keep everyone engaged in projects, it's vital to shorten the time-to-value. That means getting some early wins that keep everyone engaged in moving things forward.

Modern software can do this as long as it is built into the plan from the beginning. In our case, our goal is always to have the system configured so that deals can be priced with it inside of a month. Yes, more tweaks will be made, and we are often still finishing up integrations and data feeds, but deals can be priced and won, and benefits (and goodwill) can start accruing very early.

This heads off a lot of frustration from both users and management, and it helps keep the back end of the project on track. Getting something live and "in the wild" sooner also has the added benefit of accumulating new data. You learn what works and what still needs to be adjusted early enough to easily make the changes. It is always harder if you wait.

With that said, change is hard. We know this firsthand, and we've witnessed many banks struggle with it, as well. But positive change also brings opportunities. With the right processes in place, you'll be ready to implement those changes and vault your bank ahead of the competition.

Training: The True Test

We've now come to where the rubber meets the road. You need to roll out the new pricing system to the lenders and get them to actually use it in the way it's intended. Unfortunately, when rolling out any piece of the ecosystem of tools we described in Chapter 8, you might be fighting against some deeply held grievances.

Most lenders have had an awful pricing model inflicted upon them somewhere along the way, and they'll eye any new tool with a healthy dose of skepticism. This is one of the reasons Carl has banned the term "pricing model" when referencing our own software. He considers it a borderline fireable offense. This deeply embedded skepticism is why it's so important to involve lenders early; if they aren't part of the buying decision, you might already be too late.

To overcome this kind of bias, you will need a carefully orchestrated roll out. We consider the implementation a full-blown marketing campaign, and we put a lot of effort into the messaging. Lenders will start getting teaser emails well in advance of training, all with the intention of softening the hard feelings and building some anticipation. By the time they actually show up at their training session, the lenders should be curious about the specifics and have confidence that you are making a genuine attempt to provide them with a tool that is for their benefit, not one that will be used to police them or limit their pricing independence.

The training itself is incredibly important. The goal of this session should not be to make your lenders technical experts on the new pricing tool. Instead, the goal is to get them beyond the Price Setting issues and concerns so they are thinking about Price Getting. Training should focus on the best way for them to talk about price and structure with their borrowers, and how this new tool can facilitate that discussion.

To this end, don't lose your users by getting too far into the weeds. If you've done your job well to this point, you'll have a tool that is intuitive and easy to use and that is well supported by the vendor with lots of self-serve training and help material. Your users don't need to know what every single button in the system does, nor is that a realistic goal for training.

Here are the keys of a successful training session for any tool.

- Keep it short. No one can pay attention through a four-hour training session, no matter how good the trainer is. And lenders aren't exactly known for their long attention spans.

- Focus on the end results. Spend your training time on what the tool generates more than the "click here and check that box" technicalities. Your lenders should leave knowing what kinds of borrower conversations the tool will facilitate; they can figure out where to click to make that happen as they go. The system has been "hired" to do a job, and understanding that job is far more important than all of the ins and outs of the tool.

- Let the users take it for a test drive. They should be intrigued enough by the potential value that they are clamoring for the opportunity to play with the system. This is the only way you will really end up with fully functional users. If they need to be shown every little click they will ever make, you will end up with users who only know a small percentage of the full functionality.

- Do it in person. Strive do the training on-site if at all possible. Yes, most of these things can be done remotely via the web or by pre-recorded training videos. But the effectiveness of such virtual training options is a fraction of what can be accomplished when the training is done in person. For systems and tools this is important; it's worth spending the extra time and money to do multiple sessions to get as many people face-to-face as possible. The ROI on the technology will be far higher and will easily cover this added expense.

Who Are Your Power Users?

Another key for training is determining the individuals who absolutely must become power users. Of course, the aim will be to make all users at least proficient, but keep in mind the disproportionate production we discussed way back in Chapter 6 (What Makes a Great Lender). If your bank has a typical Zipfian distribution of loan profits, then focus your attention and resources on the dollar and quarter lenders, and not the nickel and penny lenders. Worrying about getting all users to an acceptable level of proficiency is not just difficult—it may well be impossible.

As proof, we offer up the story of Steve.

The Story of Steve

Steve was a lender at one of our early clients, and he was actually quite enthusiastic about learning the new pricing tool. He had been told how important it was to the bank, and he was nothing if not diligent. But let's just say that computers were not Steve's strong point. We fielded a steady stream of support calls from Steve that covered a wide variety of issues. They ranged from "What is my password?" to "Can you please show me again where the collateral gets entered?" One common element, though, was that Steve always politely suggested that we should include our phone number on our support site. He explained that doing so would make it far easier for him to contact us, as instead he had to keep calling the bank's Treasurer and asking for the number.

This flummoxed us because we had made certain to put the phone number on the support site. Email or direct tickets are a little more efficient for us, but we are always happy to meet our clients in whatever channel they are most comfortable with, so we had put the number prominently at the top right corner of the page from day one.

Steve, though, insisted it wasn't there, and eventually progressed from politely asking to demanding that we add it. We scrambled to figure out the problem, running a variety of browser tests and even brought in the bank's IT department. We eventually set up a screen share so that our team could see the exact same screens that Steve was seeing. As soon as it popped up on the monitor, it became painfully obvious what our problem was: Steve had, at some point, set his browser to be zoomed to +400%. For some undetermined amount of time, he had been viewing only the very top left corner of the entire Internet.

It was at this point that we realized the true extent of the task we had signed up for, which happens to be the same task you face in improving pricing. On the one hand, your very best lenders will demand a powerful tool that can handle incredibly complex structures. They intuitively know how important structure and pricing are to their customer relationships, and don't want to be told they can't quickly offer an option to a borrower because the pricing tool can't handle it.

On the other hand, you will have the Steves of the bank. They will use the tool when asked, but getting them up to speed will drain every bit of your resources. Because getting ALL lenders to use ALL of the functionality in the right way is a Herculean (maybe impossible) task, instead focus your limited resources where they will have the maximum impact: on the lenders who are generating the vast majority of the volume. As with all things related to pricing, don't let perfect be the enemy of good.

The Adoption Phase

The training of your lenders will feel like the grand finale to your project. To some extent this is true. If you have followed the playbook and executed it well, there will be immediate and significant improvements in the bank's performance. Your lenders will be using pricing as a way to build relationships instead of treating it as the necessary evil in getting a deal done. However, a true pricing transformation doesn't end with the initial roll out to the lenders.

For starters, this is pricing, which means you have a whole lot of additional stakeholders to make happy. Management will need to close the loop on all of the investments made to this point. Finance will need to see how the pricing targets are translating to production. Credit will need to figure out how they interact with what is likely a change in the order of operations.

And don't forget that all those freshly trained lenders have to actually start using the software.

In short, you have rewired the brain of the bank described in Chapter 8, and there will be some lingering pain. What you are experiencing is the critical, but often ignored, Adoption Phase. This is the point in the project where momentum must be maintained, problems must be identified and corrected, and good habits must be formed. If not? Well . . .

Every vendor has its share of adoption tales of woes and we're no exception. Here are some of the mistakes we've seen and the lessons we've learned along the way.

Creating Uneven Playing Fields

Any time a new system is implemented at your bank, there's going to be an early period in which you need to build up the trust of the system's users. They have to feel that the system is there to benefit them and make their lives easier. Nothing sabotages those efforts faster than doling out access to the system unevenly, with some lenders getting licenses and others having to share access. It creates a pricing caste system, and it makes it very hard to track performance. If your lenders don't feel you're judging their performance fairly, you've got a big problem on your hands.

Refusing to Remove the Training Wheels

Have you seen the *Seinfeld* episode where Jerry buys his father, Morty, a new handheld electronic organizer called "The Wizard"? Morty tells Jerry he loves the gift, and then proceeds to only use it for calculating tips, much to Jerry's chagrin.

Banks make the same mistake when they purchase a pricing tool and then only let the lenders do the bare minimum with it. By failing to trust and empower their lenders, they're basically heading down the same path Ryan took in Chapter 7, which ended with the lenders rebelling against the pricing tool (and Ryan).

If you're not willing to give your lenders that level of freedom, then you either need to refrain from buying the software or bring in some new lenders who will inspire more confidence.

Putting the Cart Before the Horse

This doesn't happen too often, but we have seen banks get so excited about the potential of a new pricing tool that they put one in place before they have a pressing need for it, i.e., enough lenders to leverage the tool's power or a large enough commercial book to impact the bank's bottom line.

It's great to be looking ahead when it comes to technology. Just don't look too far ahead.

Setting It (Up) and Forgetting It

It's sorely tempting to stop and take a break after pushing through the purchasing, implementing, and training phases. Don't do it.

At this stage you're being watched very carefully by your lenders. Chances are they feel a bit jaded when it comes to new software. They've probably experienced at least one "next great thing" that never got any traction at the bank. So they'll be looking for signals from bank management when the new pricing tool comes out.

If you fail to provide incentives for putting the new software to use or you don't make it clear that there will be repercussions if the software isn't used, then you're sending a loud message to your lenders. It says: "We're not really that invested in the success of this software."

If management's not going to buy in, then why should the lenders?

Getting Incentives Right

Of course, you can't just dangle any old carrot in front of your lenders and expect the right results. To ensure your pricing overhaul is successful, you might just need to overhaul the incentive compensation for your lenders, as well.

There are countless examples of incentives gone bad, leading to unethical behavior. But most banks are actually pretty good at this. They have enough controls and balances in place to avoid truly ugly ethical scandals. Instead, banks more often fall victim to the law of unintended consequences.

The most common example of this is found in the call center. The call center staff is measured on number of calls answered or average call length. Yes, you get the efficiency you're after, but you also get an awful experience for your customers as the staff plays hot potato with the issue, quickly (and rudely) passing off anything difficult instead of taking ownership of the problem and solving it for the customer.

Unfortunately, these kinds of misaligned incentives can crop up everywhere in banks. Dallas ran across dozens of them in his banker days, including a few incredibly common situations that are real head scratchers.

For example, most banks incentivize their tellers to have balanced drawers. At the end of a week or month, any teller who has had a balanced drawer for the entire period will receive a small bonus. Dallas saw tellers spend hours searching for where they got off by a dime. Not only was this lost labor, but it also caused long customer lines as tellers helped each other look for mistakes during shift changes or day changeovers. All for the sake of a dime.

In another bank, the credit analysts were measured on the number of credit memos they generated in a month. As you can imagine, the memos were sloppy, and important red flags were missed. Even worse, this system also ensured that the large, complex deals, the time-consuming ones you'd want to avoid in this incentive system, ended up in the hands of the people without enough clout to pawn them off on someone else—i.e., the most junior analysts. The bank's most critical deals were being underwritten by kids who were weeks out of college instead of by experienced experts. Not surprisingly, this bank got waylaid with some huge losses during the financial crisis.

The bottom line is that incentives matter, and they need to be well thought out. As commercial lending is the biggest source of both profit and risk in the bank, surely the incentive plans there have been perfected, right? Not even close. We see two mistakes on a regular basis that tend to do more harm than good.

It's All about Size

Most lenders are incented on the size of their loan portfolio. Period. Yes, banks are probably measuring lots of other things, including spreads, fee income, deposit balances, and loss rates. In most banks, however, lenders know that this is just noise. When it comes time for raises, bonuses, and promotions, it is all about the size of the portfolio. Did you grow your portfolio by $25 million last year? Then no one will say much about the relative risk or profitability levels, and your bonus is safe.

There are obvious problems with this mindset, and most bankers are fully aware of them. They know that lenders will do anything to avoid adding friction when a loan is on the verge of closing. Asking for that extra collateral, or the personal guarantee, or to move the deposit balances is an afterthought at best.

So why does this approach persist? The answer is essentially that it is easy. Portfolio balance is the one number that every lender knows, and as it does have a positive correlation with profitability, why not use it? Just remember that as in all industries, you get what you pay for. If you pay for loan growth, you'll get it, but usually at the expense of profitability, or risk management, or both.

Getting Too Metric Happy

The second big mistake we see is a result of the effort to avoid misaligned incentives and unintended consequences. In trying to close all of the loopholes, banks end up incentivizing lenders on almost everything associated with their deals. Bonuses get calculated using a massive spreadsheet that combines loan growth, loss rates, cross selling, duration, prepayments, and anything else the bank can think of to throw in. If you measure and incent on too many things to keep track of, then you really aren't measuring anything. It has to be simple and straightforward.

The good news is that risk-based pricing will give you just that metric: a number that incents the right kind of behavior without sacrificing profitability or safety. For every deal you price, and for every account already on the books, you calculate a risk-adjusted net income. This number takes the good parts of measuring portfolio balances (the fact that more loans usually means more income) but removes the temptation to add unprofitable deals, bad structures, or risky credits. They all get dinged too much by the risk adjustments to benefit the lender.

By measuring lenders on an income number, you can get them to start thinking like owners of the business. Their portfolio becomes their own little enterprise, where they try to maximize their income each period but with an awareness that all their actions have repercussions that matter.

Taking a Short-Term Approach

Finally, we'll leave you with one last lesson we've learned on aligning incentives with the desired behaviors. When you get access to all of the incredible data that pricing and profitability tools generate, the temptation is to use it as the nominal starting point to make all decisions. If you see that Bob has the most profitable portfolio, the temptation will be to focus on Bob to the exclusion of your other lenders when it comes to bonus or promotion time. The same is true for profitable customers.

We have found, however, that measuring trends tends to be far more powerful than measuring absolute levels. For any sector of your business, any customer, or any lender, you should aim for incremental progress toward your ultimate goal. This is a surprisingly effective framework, and worth digging into a lot deeper. That's where we'll head for Chapter 11.

CHAPTER 11: THE POWER OF CONTINUOUS IMPROVEMENT

"The journey of 1,000 miles begins with a single step." — Lao Tzu

"Forget about perfection; focus on progression, and compound the improvements."

— Sir Dave Brailsford, British cycling coach

To get your bank where it needs to go, all you have to do is change its pricing culture, create a new C-level position, break down silos, share more information, create a new ecosystem of tools, figure out which tools to purchase, and then get everyone to use them once they're put in place.

If that last sentence just made your eye start twitching or led you to curl up in a fetal position in the corner of your office, we understand. If it seems overwhelming, that's because it is . . . but it's only overwhelming if you think of it in those terms, as one huge, gargantuan undertaking. If you take the advice of Lao Tzu and Dave Brailsford, though, you'll have a place to start and a path to follow.

At the risk of being repetitive, let's go back to what we wrote in Chapter 2, when we introduced the concept of "Price Getting."

As much as it pains bankers, when it comes to Price Setting, they need to live by the old saying, "Don't let perfect be the enemy of good." Pricing is a forward-looking, prospective exercise, and, as such, it can get messy.

There is no such thing as 100% accuracy, and bankers (especially the finance types) get uncomfortable with the uncertainty. They know the importance of pricing, so there is an urge to get the assumptions just right. And many, like Frankenstein Bank, will spend years trying to get everything perfected. In the meantime, they are pricing millions of dollars in loans with an old tool they know is flawed.

Instead, banks should use a "continuous deployment" mentality, whereby they can roll out the improved methodology—after all, it is better than what you have!—and slowly refine it over time. All of this should happen with the understanding that perfection is not the goal. There will come a point when gaining the extra degree of accuracy is not worth the time, resources, or interference with end users needed to achieve it.

Nice words, to be sure, but to bring them from theory to reality, you need a framework. That's where Dave Brailsford and the story of the British Cycling Team can help.

What British Cycling Can Teach Your Bank

Things may be tough in banking right now, but chances are your bank is in much better shape than British cycling was in 2002.

That's when Dave Brailsford took over the program. In the 76 years before Brailsford came on board, the British track cycling team had won a grand total of one Olympic gold medal. Just six years later, the Brits dominated track cycling at the 2008 Olympic Games in Beijing, winning seven of the 10 available gold medals. Four years later they replicated the feat in London. Meanwhile, in 2010 Brailsford undertook a similar challenge with the British professional road cycling team, Team Sky. Just two years later, the team produced the first-ever British winner of the Tour de France, beginning a string of three British winners in five years.

How did Brailsford improve British cycling from irrelevant to dominant? One percent at a time.

The Theory of Marginal Gains

When Brailsford took over British cycling, he was well aware of just how far removed the program was from reaching the top of the podium in the Olympics. To avoid being overwhelmed by the task at hand, he went back to some of the process-improvement research he'd read about while getting his MBA.

"It struck me that we should think small, not big," Brailsford said in a Harvard Business Review interview[13]. "Adopt a philosophy of continuous improvement through the aggregation of marginal gains. Forget about perfection; focus on progression, and compound the improvements."

Brailsford and his team were relentless in seeking out all the ways they could make small, steady gains. They did everything from improving hand washing to avoid illnesses at events, to keeping the mechanics area at the track free of dust. Equipment, aerodynamic positioning on the bike, power needed at the start of a race—British cycling looked at all sorts of ways in which they could get just a little bit better, and a little bit closer to gold.

Don't Confuse the Peas for the Steaks

It wasn't that straightforward, of course. The marginal gains needed to be made in the right areas—"the steak" as Brailsford put it—and not on the periphery, or "the peas." That was a mistake Brailsford admitted to making

---

[13]   Harrell, Eben. "How 1% Performance Improvements Led to Olympic Gold." Harvard Business Review. N.p., 30 Oct. 2015. Web. 17 Feb. 2017. <https://hbr.org/2015/10/how-1-performance-improvements-led-to-olympic-gold>.

initially when he switched from running a track program to a professional road cycling team. Poor results in the first few races helped the team realize they were concerned about too many bells and whistles and that they needed to shift the focus of their efforts.

"If you don't know what you're aiming for, you're never going to get there." – Sir Dave Brailsford

Is the Gap Bridgeable?

Even if the improvements are made in the right areas, they need to be able to add up to the desired result. For British cycling, that meant medal-winning performance. Cyclists whom they felt could be improved to that level made the cut. Those whose gap between their current status and their future goal was too wide were dropped.

What's Your Bank's Benchmark?

So what would this look like if you tried it at your bank? You'd start with where you want your bank to go in the future.

"If you don't know what you're aiming for, you're never going to get there," Brailsford said in a 2015 talk he gave at the Investors in People Outperformance Roadshow[14]. "Get a true understanding of what it's going to take to get there, then come back and do an audit."

Remember this chart from Chapter 5?

---

[14] Investors In People. "Investors in People - Sir Dave Brailsford, Outperformance Roadshow." YouTube. YouTube, 30 Mar. 2015. Web. 17 Feb. 2017. <https://www.youtube.com/watch?v=bG3WeIkMTKQ>.

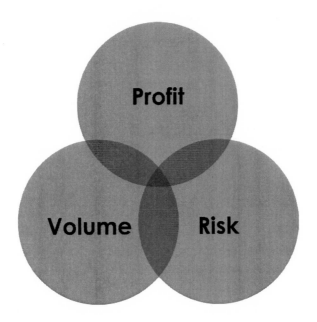

Figuring out where you want your bank to fall in this diagram can be a helpful way for a bank to determine its goals. The mark you plan to reach needs to be quantifiable. Vague platitudes like "We want faster growth and more profits." won't get you anywhere. Something like "We want to grow our portfolio by 15% without sacrificing margins." gives you a much clearer goal.

"Boy is it easy to do an audit once you know what you're benchmarking against," Brailsford said.

Identify the Steak

The big juicy T-bone of potential improvement at your bank isn't cost-cutting or compliance, it's revenue. There you'll find numerous places—the customer experience, pricing, etc.—where you can make those marginal improvements that served British cycling so well. A small increase of basis points on certain loans, a tiny improvement in the number of deals you win each month, a slightly shorter duration on some of your loans, a gradual streamlining of the loan decision-making process . . . the list can go on and on.

Those cost-cutting moves? They're the peas. As we noted back in Chapter 1, McKinsey & Co. made that point back in 2003 in their influential article, "The Power of Pricing." In its research of S&P 1500 companies, McKinsey found that a 1% increase in pricing had an impact on profits that was "nearly 50% greater than that of a 1% fall in variable costs such as materials and direct labor."

Become a Positive Place

Brailsford believes that once the marginal gain process gets rolling, "it creates a contagious enthusiasm. Everyone starts looking for ways to improve . . . . Our team became a very positive place to be."

Banks can become that positive place. They can set ambitious goals for the future and reach them. They just need to identify where they can improve and then start making gains, 1% at a time.

Continuous Improvement, Portfolio Level

Where can those potential improvements be found at your bank? On two levels, transactional and portfolio.

Let's start on the portfolio level. Bear with us here as we again go to an example outside banking to make our point.

OODA Loop

During the Korean War, American fighter pilots were outnumbered and outgunned.

At the time, the U.S. Air Force's state-of-the-art fighter jet was the F-86 Sabre, and the North Koreans were using the Soviet produced MiG-15. The MiG-15 was the world's first swept-wing fighter, and it had superior range, speed, turning radius, climbing ability, and weapons. However, despite flying in what appeared to all experts to be inferior equipment, the U.S. Sabre pilots racked up a kill ratio of nearly 14:1 against the MiGs in the world's first all-jet dogfights.

What was it about the American pilots that allowed them to completely dominate with slower planes? The answer may surprise you, and it can teach us a lot about how the world's highest-performing banks are putting distance between themselves and the competition.

One of the brash young pilots of those F-86 Sabres was John Boyd. After the war he sought an explanation for the lopsided kill ratio. He found that, while the MiG-15 was superior in the ways planes had traditionally been measured, the F-86 Sabres had two important differences. First, they had a large canopy with clear visibility in all directions. Second, they had a hydraulic boost to the flight control system (the "stick" in pilot terms).

These two advantages allowed the American pilots to better see what the enemy was doing and start counter-maneuvers. By the time the enemy reacted, they would be starting a new maneuver. The enemy was reacting too slowly to old information, and after several iterations, they would find a Sabre close on their tail in the kill zone.

Boyd took this insight and perfected a new technique. He became an instructor at the exclusive Fighter Weapons School (FWS), which was basically Top Gun in the late 1950s. Most of the world's best pilots eventually came through FWS, and Boyd had a standing bet for all of them. Starting from a position of disadvantage, Boyd would have any taker dead in his sights in less than 40 seconds, a bet he called "40 seconds for 40 bucks." In reality, he rarely needed more than 20 seconds, but Boyd liked the idea of winning $40 a lot more than winning $20. In more than 3,000 hours of flight time at FWS, Boyd never lost his bet. He was a combination of John Wayne and Doc Holliday.

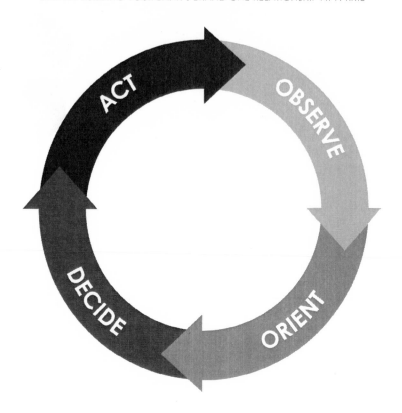

Boyd formalized his approach, which he called the "Boyd Cycle." It later became known as the "OODA Loop," which stands for Observe, Orient, Decide, and Act. The OODA Loop became (and still is) the standard for all fighter pilots and has since been used in broader military and business strategy.

The basic concept is that if you can "get inside" the competition's loop, you can quickly form a hypothesis, test it, observe results, and form another hypothesis before the competitor can get through their first loop. Instead of worrying about getting the action exactly perfect, the goal is to quickly make the best possible decision and test the outcome. More iterations will get to the right outcome much faster (and better) than stubbornly trying to perfect a hypothesis before it ever goes to market.

For example, in the software business, instead of spending 18 months perfecting the next release (all while the market continues to evolve) and finding out your product isn't exactly what customers want, the successful companies are making their best guess at what customers want, building a minimum viable product quickly, and then releasing it to be tested. That minimal product can then be perfected and improved in stages, all with constant feedback from real paying customers.

How does this compare to the banking world? Are banks good at making quick decisions and learning from them?

Paralysis by Analysis

We recently saw a classic example of what this process looks like in a bank we'll call First Paralysis. This particular institution is a well-known and respected regional bank with more than $20 billion in total assets. Their performance has been inconsistent of late, and the focus of nearly every quarterly earnings call has been the competitive marketplace and pricing pressure across all business lines. Management was tired of missing both earnings and growth estimates and was curious about the impact of meeting the pricing of some of their more aggressive competition. In banking, when a question like this is asked, the finance team springs into action.

First Paralysis paid a third party for in-depth surveys of average market pricing by product in each of their markets. A team of analysts then compared that market data to all of the bank's deals that had been booked in the last two years, running regressions to find the pricing that would have generated optimal pricing to maximize growth and earnings. The result, after six months of work, was an impressive 96-page document detailing a back-tested model that met all of their thresholds for statistical significance. Based on about a dozen variables, they claimed they knew how to adjust pricing in the future to optimize results.

Despite the heft of this impressive document, though, it contained a few fatal flaws.

First, no one on the senior management team was able to wade through the entire report. It was mind-numbingly boring and strayed way too far from reality into theory. Management simply wasn't comfortable making decisions derived from a model they couldn't understand or easily explain.

Second, the analysis was completely stale. Two of First Paralysis' primary competitors had merged, rates had moved, elections were on the horizon, regulations had been added, and on top of all that, there had been a shakeup on the senior management team. So even if the analysis had not been based on retrofitted decisions from the prior two years, the bank was still reacting to the competition's old strategies.

In short, their OODA loop was way too long and slow to be effective.

The vast majority of banks make decisions this way. Just by the nature of the business, bankers are generally more concerned about being wrong (and losing money) than being right (and at best getting paid back with a small interest rate). The incentives of a highly leveraged business make bankers overly cautious.

In many cases, this is the right approach, such as when making credit decisions. But what about rolling out new technology? Or trying new products? Or changing loan and deposit pricing? All of these decisions should be made the same way John Boyd engaged enemy pilots. Form a hypothesis, quickly test it, and learn from the result. Wash, rinse, and repeat.

For First Paralysis, that would have been as simple as choosing a few products in a few of their markets and reducing pricing. Gauge the change in volume relative to all of the other markets, and quickly learn how demand changes. That results in nearly real-time feedback, and those experiments should be running constantly to find the pricing "sweet spot" in an ever-evolving marketplace. Of course, that also means you need to re-wire the decision-making process once you have that information.

Waiting until the next quarterly ALCO meeting to enact pricing decisions creates a long, unwieldy OODA Loop that can easily be exploited by the competition. Instead, you need someone manning the pricing controls, i.e., the Chief Pricing Officer (Chapter 5), who will use the data generated by the tools in the pricing ecosystem to make quick decisions. The ALCO meetings should be used to discuss the results of all of those little tests and to give the CPO guidance on the bank's high-level strategy.

Bankers can generally get on board with the incremental improvement concept at the portfolio level, but they often feel that it doesn't apply to individual transactions. After all, "the market is the market," and there is only so much room to deviate from the competition, right?

Actually . . .

Continuous Improvement at the Transaction Level

Early in our discussions with almost every bank, we have some version of this exchange.

Bank: Can you show us how you change the hurdle rates?

Us: Actually, we don't use hurdle rates. We think you should use targets instead.

Sometimes it feels like we can actually hear the eyes roll over the phone. We know exactly what they're thinking. "Yeah, whatever, that's just semantics from the pricing nerds." This is far more than just semantics—in fact, this subtle change in mindset actually has a transformative effect on decision making and performance.

The Case Against Hurdles

Let's start by talking about why we don't use hurdles. It's a long list, so we'll summarize it.

Hurdle rates are, by definition, the absolute lowest return the bank will accept on a deal. Is this really the number you want driving all the pricing decisions in your bank? If you have a hurdle, it should be treated as a state secret that requires security clearance. Publishing them or, even worse, using them as the guidepost on your pricing system results in two substantial problems.

First, if this is truly a hurdle rate, you take all flexibility (and common sense) away from your lenders. We recently saw an instance in which a lender was working on a deal for one of the bank's most profitable customers and, due to competitive offers, was a few basis points short of meeting the hurdle rate. Those few basis points translated to about $200 per year, but as it didn't meet the hurdle, the lender couldn't meet the critical terms.

As we all know, deals are rarely priced in a vacuum. The competing bank started cross-selling, and pretty soon the entire relationship was at stake, representing nearly $250,000 of annual profits, all because of a refusal to bend a few basis point on one deal.

That scenario is exactly why the term "pricing model" has been banned in the PrecisionLender offices. When you think of your platform as a "model," you treat "hurdle rates" as the gospel. That removes all ability for experienced lenders to negotiate deals within the context of very complex and unique circumstances.

Even if your bank is not strictly dogmatic about hurdle rates, there is still a second major issue. If you aim at the hurdle rate on all of your deals, guess what? That's exactly what you'll get on the majority of them.

This chart, sent to us by a client, summarizes the monthly results from their old hurdle-based pricing tool. Can you guess what the hurdle rate was?

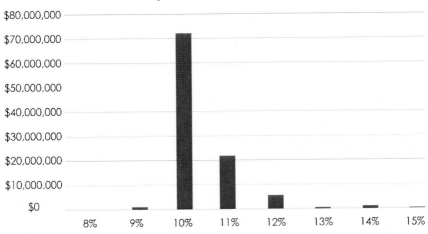

As a hurdle is a minimum return that will be accepted, it generally has to be set well below current market rates. Otherwise, volume will dry up completely. However, once that low hurdle has been set, it acts as a magnet for all of your production, drawing each deal as close to that hurdle as the lender can possibly get it. Get a couple of banks in a market to start doing this and you can imagine the results. It is one of the biggest reasons why net interest margin for U.S. banks has declined so much since the mid '90s.

Set Your Sights Higher Than "Acceptable"

If hurdle rates aren't the answer, then what should you be using? We believe wholeheartedly in using profitability targets. You are measuring the same thing (risk-adjusted return on capital), but the mindset is completely different. Targets are not set as the bare minimum that will be accepted. Instead, they are just as advertised: the target at which you are aiming. Ideally, you will find the current market level for a specific loan type and then set the target slightly above that. This ensures both that you are competitive in the local market and that you are also pushing lenders to stretch every deal just a little. You'll ask for a couple more basis points, or perhaps a little more collateral, a slightly shorter term, or for another account or two. Trying to reach those targets will make us incrementally better, deal by deal. On the typical bank volume, that soon translates to big dollars.

The bank we referenced above is small (about $2 billion in assets) and is booking about $100 million per month in loans. Those couple of basis points translate to nearly $250,000 per year in additional interest income.

Stretching Requires Flexibility

Targets should be a bit of a stretch, just above what the competitors are likely offering, but they should be paired with significantly more flexibility.

First, you want to give lenders lots of options in how they can reach those targets. Again, this is not just about rate, but about all deal terms that will move the needle in terms of risk and profit. Second, there will inevitably be times when the right business decision is to book a deal below the target. Maybe the deal is for an existing customer that is highly profitable, or maybe it's the "foot in the door" for a growing prospect that will pay off the down the road.

Whatever the reason, banks must trust their lenders. Commercial loans are complex, and each has nuances that cannot be easily captured in one profitability metric. That context and judgment is precisely why lenders are well paid; it is their job, not only to build relationships, but to structure each new deal in a way that makes sense for both the customer and the bank. Using concrete hurdle rates restricts that flexibility, and does so with the added pain of lower returns.

Trusting your lenders to be flexible allows them to channel their inner John Boyd. Back in Chapter 4 we described the benefits of moving the decision-making process closer to the customer. This faster, more efficient process allows your lenders to outmaneuver competitors on individual deals. With clearly defined targets, they know how they can adjust deal terms to meet customer needs.

For example, consider a deal where a competitor is offering a lower rate, but is doing so by shortening the amortization schedule and requiring additional guarantees. And that guarantee just happens to be from the borrower's father-in-law. Your lender should be able to quickly offer several alternatives, allowing the borrower to remove the pain points, which in this case is most likely that guarantee. Your borrower might be willing to pay a slightly higher rate to have a more comfortable Thanksgiving dinner with the in-laws.

The typical competitive bank will take weeks to respond with a counter-offer, and if they do, your lender can again instantly react to that offer. Borrowers eventually figure out which bank is being responsive, creative, and helpful, and will get tired of waiting for something better to come along from the competition. Even when challenged by competitors with superior product offerings or lower funding costs, your lenders have that one key advantage: the ability to see what the enemy is doing and quickly change course.

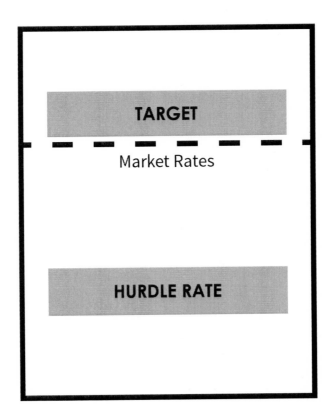

So, yes, insisting on saying "targets" instead of "hurdles" may be a bit of semantics from the pricing nerds, but this subtle change in phrasing and approach can have a massive impact at both the lender level and the bank level. Thus, we believe it's worth being a stickler on it.

Conclusion

In many ways, managing a bank can feel like trying to steer an aircraft carrier. It is an asset-based business, meaning the vast majority of today's earnings are based on decisions you made several quarters or years in the past. Correcting even small issues can seem daunting, but turning around a bank with poor earnings or a bad reputation in the market often seems impossible.

The lesson from Dave Brailsford and the British cycling team, though, is that small, continuous improvements can get you to the end goal. It just takes a little time and perseverance.

In 2013, a community bank in Oklahoma sat at a crossroads familiar to much of the industry. Although they weren't in any imminent danger, they also didn't see a clear path to continued growth. Competition in their market had become brutal, and their commercial loan portfolio was shrinking, both in terms of balance and yields. Historically, they had weathered a period like this with their residential lending arm, but with regulatory changes, much of that volume was also gone. Margins were declining, and the management team was contemplating a sale.

The bank was family-owned, however, and the chairman was a proud man who didn't want to see the bank sold on his watch. They decided instead to embark on a pricing and process overhaul for commercial lending. The start was slow and frustrating, but when the results started coming in, they saw the upside of being an asset-based business. Once they got forward momentum, the positive results started compounding, and the financial performance since then speaks for itself.

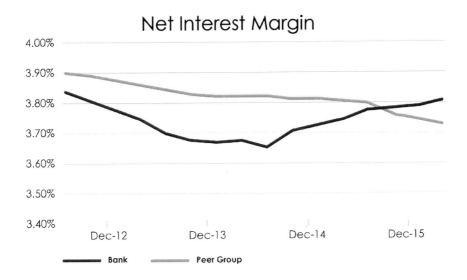

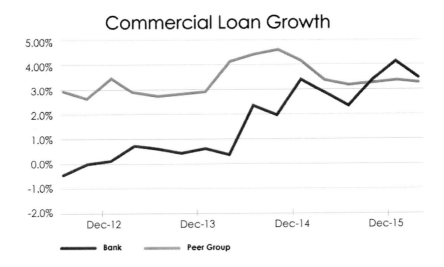

The bank transformed from a slow fade to black into a dynamic growth story, all with better earnings. They shifted from contemplating a sale to shopping for other small banks, and have since more than doubled in size. They're proof that taking that first small step, and then continuously improving, can truly transform a bank, even in the current environment.

Don't have the right pricing tool? Then go out and get one—they're out there. (See Chapter 9: Choosing the Right Tool.)

Don't trust your lenders enough? Then teach them how to be better lenders—or find new ones. (See Chapter 6: What Makes a Great Lender?)

Don't think your bank can change? The reread this chapter. Change doesn't have to happen all at once, just a little bit a time.

The good news? Every little bit counts, sometimes more than you know.

CHAPTER 12: HOW WILL YOU "*EARN IT*" IN THE FUTURE?

> Artificial Intelligence allows computers to do what they do best, so humans can do what they do best—foster and maintain important relationships.

Up to this point we've talked about how your bank needs to "*Earn It.*" We've walked you through the importance of building relationships, the central role pricing plays, and how those relationships build your bank's all-important brand.

But that's all about where your bank needs to go now. When you get there, where will your bank go next?

Why Banks Should Really, Really Care About AI

The banking industry we all know today has been shaped by a handful of key transformations. There was the formation of the FDIC in the 1930s to restore public faith in banks. Then there was the phasing out of Regulation Q interest rate ceilings on deposit accounts in the 1980s. In 1994, the Riegle-Neal Interstate Banking Act relaxed restrictions against interstate branching. Then there was the explosive growth of online and mobile banking over the last two decades that has reshaped the way banks deliver their products and interact with their customers. Now we are on the brink of another generational transformation with machine learning and artificial intelligence (AI).

(Note: While there are definitional differences between artificial intelligence and machine learning, for the purposes of simplicity, we'll use the term "AI" in this chapter.)

Many bankers will dismiss this notion as just the latest "trend of the day" among technology firms. After all, bankers have been exposed to many fear-mongering sales pitches, and they've learned to ignore the doomsday "Your business is about to change!" kind of messaging. This time it's different, however, because AI is exploding in every industry and in countless different use cases.

A go-to example, and one you're probably already familiar with, is the self-driving car, but AI is also at the root of many tools and products you use on a daily basis. Amazon, for example, uses AI to predict what products you will want to see, based on what you're already viewing, what you've purchased in the past, and what others with similar context have purchased. And Amazon is exceptionally good at it.

Similar approaches are used by Spotify to suggest what music you will like, by Apple to predict which apps you will buy, by Google to hone the perfect search results, and by Facebook to shape your personal news feed. There are other subtle examples, as well. Have you noticed airline confirmation emails now automatically generate calendar events for the flights? Have you seen your iPhone or Facebook photo collections organized by the people in the pictures?

These things happen behind the scenes and are rarely noticed or thought about by end users, but they have been game-changers for each of the aforementioned companies. They are now taking that success and pushing AI front and center in our lives in the form of Siri, Alexa, Cortana, Google Assistant, and the like. These "bots" are powered by AI, and the more interaction we have with them, the better they "learn" how to respond to human voice commands and accurately and efficiently answer queries.

As the possibilities for AI expand, the list of industries it can impact will grow. In fact, banking might be the perfect business for AI. To understand why, we need to go back a few years to a story that will be familiar to many experienced bankers.

Ed to the Rescue

"These 'bots' are powered by AI, and the more interaction we have with them, the better they 'learn' how to respond to human voice commands…"

Years ago, Dallas had the good fortune to work for a bank with pristine credit quality. This squeaky-clean portfolio was fiercely protected by Ed, who was one of those classic, old-school credit guys. Ed had minimal formal credit training, and the bank didn't rely on any sophisticated modeling or algorithms for monitoring risk. Instead, they relied on Ed's gut instincts.

Ed had a way of sniffing out bad deals, and several team members looked forward to the weekly loan committee meeting, during which Ed would tear into the latest poor sap that dared to bring a wobbly deal for approval. After one of the more contentious meetings, Ed was asked how he was able to quickly spot tiny flaws that the analysts had missed after hours of work, and why he was such a stickler about them.

"I learned this business in the 80s, and had to help clean up two banks before I was 40. The bad news was I missed way too much time with my family. The good news was that I saw firsthand every conceivable way a deal could bite you in the ass. And I've decided that I am NEVER doing another clean up."

Ed couldn't always put his finger on why a deal was bad, but he had learned to trust himself when something just felt "off." The bank passed on a lot of deals based on those feelings, and their competitors gladly jumped on them. A whole lot of them ended up defaulting.

Obviously Ed isn't some kind of Nostradamus of banking. Instead, he was spotting patterns and correlations, even if he was doing it subconsciously. He knew he'd seen similar situations before, and they had ended badly. Most banks used to be run this way. It was one of those approaches that worked well . . . until it didn't.

When Ed's Not Enough

Some banks didn't have quite as good a version of Ed. Some banks outgrew their Ed, growing large enough that they couldn't give the personal smell test to every single deal. Much of the industry simply ran out of enough Eds who had cut their teeth in the bad times. A lot of banks were using an Ed who had never seen a true credit correction.

The real issue is that humans are actually pretty bad at spotting and acting on patterns. Our lizard brain (a term we discussed earlier in Chapter 6) is the part of the mind responsible for our instinctive reactions, like "fight or flight." It leads us astray far more often than we realize. This was true even for Ed's bank; he may have kept our portfolio safe, but he did so at a huge opportunity cost. The growth the bank eked out was slow and painful, and being a stickler on quality meant they passed on a lot of profitable business.

The Faulty Lizard Brain

So how could the very thing that made Ed so valuable—his ability to use limited and ambiguous data to make an instinctive prediction—also turn out to be a problem? Because when you lean heavily on gut instinct you open yourself up to multiple cognitive biases that also make their homes in the lizard brain. A few are particularly prevalent in banking.

Confirmation Bias

This is the natural tendency of people to favor information that confirms their preexisting belief or hypothesis. In fact, you not only favor this confirming information, you actually seek it out at the exclusion of any contradictory information. Those perpetual market bears who always see a crash around the corner (and yes, every office has at least one) seek out ugly data that confirm that expectation, and they are much more likely to remember and believe that data than any positive economic data they might find. It's become an easier trap to fall into in today's world, with its unlimited and easily accessible supply of data and opinions.

Sunk-Cost Bias

Instead of being ignored, sunk costs (those costs that have already been incurred and cannot be recovered), are often a major driving force in determining ongoing strategy at banks. You've probably heard one of these maddening arguments before:

- We spent X dollars on the software, so we are sticking with it even though it is clearly not the best solution.

- We took those advances to hedge those specific loans, so we cannot pay them off early.

- We started moving rates down last month, so we can't move them up this month.

- We have invested too much time and money in that branch to close it.

You get the idea.

Incentives Bias

This is pretty straightforward: Humans figure out the type of behavior that's rewarded and then shape their behavior accordingly. If you put in a compensation system that rewards lenders for growth, then you're going to get a bias toward closing deals. Sometimes that's fine, but often that means the bank winds up with some questionable, high-risk loans on its books. Flip the script and reward lenders for minimizing risk and you'll get high-quality deals . . . but not very many of them. Finding the right balance with incentives is tricky; failure to do so leads to short-term behaviors that are detrimental in the long run.

Inertia Bias

Or as Carl calls it, the "We've always done it this way" bias.

It's maddening but, sadly, not uncommon. Case in point: Carl's had several discussions with banks that are having an issue with loans leaving the bank through natural amortization. When he brings up the idea of switching those customers to an interest-only loan he often gets this response:

"We never thought of it that way . . . but we can never do that because folks believe that you just have to amortize things."

You may have just chuckled a bit, but if you give it some thought, chances are you've got an example of inertia bias in your bank as well.

Eds Everywhere

Despite all those potential traps set by the lizard brain, the story of Ed probably still rings true for a lot of bankers. The surprising thing isn't that some banks still handle credit risk this way; it's how many other kinds of decisions are handled in the exact same manner. Most banks have an Ed for credit, for pricing, for investments, for security, and for every other significant function they handle. And almost all of them are, when you get right down to it, flying by the seat of their pants.

Other businesses look like this, too. A doctor diagnoses based on both the latest medical tests and their own judgment, which has been honed over hundreds or thousands of similar cases. A lawyer suggests legal strategy based on precedent and their own case history.

In each of these examples, however, the human is limited by two things. First, how many experiences do they have that fit the exact same criteria? Usually it numbers in the dozens or low hundreds, and it's not enough to be statistically significant. Second, are they pulling off the Herculean task of avoiding all the cruel tricks our minds play on us? The lizard brain is a powerful foe to overcome.

The Beauty of Cold Calculation

This brings us back to AI. Humans may be limited in spotting patterns, but luckily you have help in the form of computers, which were literally created to do just this.

Your best, most experienced bankers might see a particular type of loan a few hundred times in their career. A computer with access to a decent data set can review a few hundred thousand in a split second. It will find patterns that you miss, and it won't be subject to all of your little flaws. Now you aren't even required to have your experienced humans build software that knows how to spot a bad deal. Just like Siri and Cortana, it will learn that all on its own.

Why Now? (A Brief History of AI)

AI may seem like a futuristic technology that is just now taking shape, but it was actually born in the 1950s, when famed cryptologist and computer scientist Alan Turing started teaching computers to carry on conversations. That soon led to AI becoming an official field of research at Dartmouth College in 1956. After massive funding cuts in the 1970s created what came to be called "the AI winter," the field eventually emerged to show progress in the mid-1980s and again in the mid-1990s.

The technology started to become more mainstream in 1997 when IBM's Deep Blue defeated Garry Kasparov in chess. A later IBM creation, Watson, learned how to play (and win) the game show *Jeopardy* in 2011. In 2016, Google's AI finally achieved what many thought was the final frontier in human gaming superiority by beating Lee Sodol at the game Go. While these feats were newsworthy, they were also somewhat trivial. They were achieved by academic types, and had more of a parlor trick feel than a real, purposeful application.

The technology wasn't all that complicated, it was just that there were two severe bottlenecks.

First, computing power was too scarce. Cranking through millions of computations in a short time required enormous computing power, and only a few places in the world had access to enough of that power to really make it work. Second, there weren't very many data sets worthy of machine learning. Data storage was prohibitively expensive, so most data was abandoned to the ether. Both of these limitations are quickly eroding.

The proliferation of cloud computing has made growing amounts of processing power and data storage available for mere pennies. Today it's cheaper to store all data than it is to take the time deciding which data are important and which can be thrown out. Because of this, there are now enormous untapped piles of data sitting all over the world. Anyone with a valid credit card can access Microsoft Azure or Amazon's AWS and spin up as many servers as needed to power any conceivable software. With all that horsepower and raw material (data) available, computers are able to learn like never before.

Why Banks?

While this technology is being embedded everywhere, banking might be the industry in which AI can have the greatest impact.

The Data Is Already There

We hear almost daily from bankers that their data "is messy" and isn't organized well enough to be useful. Well, that simply isn't true. Banking data is some of the best-organized data on the planet. All banks have been storing similar data for decades in mostly consistent formats, and in systems that all look alike. True, those systems are old and difficult to interact with (for example, using codes like "102" to represent "Wall Street Prime" to save a little memory), and the data often sits in disconnected silos, but exists, and it's in digital form. Think about the state of the data for most of your customers. What kind of long-term historical data do your real estate developers, attorneys, or doctors have?

Banking is a treasure trove of useful data, just waiting for the right solutions to combine all of those separate sources. Once the data is combined, AI can start mining for trends and relationships between variables you never knew existed. When banks start taking data they'd previously used only for processing transactions and start using it to deliver intelligence back into their systems, a whole new world of possibilities opens up. They can go from simply looking at outcomes to looking at the choices that were made along the way and why. Then they can use that information to determine what to do in the future in similar circumstances.

In AI, Context Is King

Have you ever asked Siri to tell you a joke? Or tried to get specific information about a local restaurant? Sometimes the results are phenomenal, and you get exactly the answer you were looking for no typing required. Other times? Not so much.

The reason is that this technology is really hard to execute. Apple has to start with some idea of what users might ask. Then, yes, Siri can learn from all of those subsequent interactions, but the list of possible initial questions and tasks is literally limitless. They have to be prepared for anything because someone will eventually ask Siri for it.

In banking, however, you have much better context. For starters, any bots or intelligent digital assistants you create won't need to be able to tell a joke or choose a restaurant. They will be dealing with something pretty darned specific, i.e., financial transactions. They'll have contextual information for the user, in the form of financial statements and their previous relationship with the bank. When you narrow the potential fields so that you're only answering questions about commercial banking, the level of AI difficulty drops considerably.

Banking Relies on Judgment Calls From Experienced Executives

When you boil it down to its core, banking is really the business of risk. You spend your days answering one fundamental question: How much and what kinds of risks are involved in this transaction, and is the return sufficient to justify the allocation of capital?

Bankers have spent decades building ever more sophisticated tools for measuring and monitoring risk, but eventually, in every meaningful transaction, a human makes a decision to answer that specific question. No matter how fancy the algorithm, or how many tabs on the spreadsheet, a person is deciding based on a combination of those model outputs and their own personal experience. Again, like our friend Ed, how many deals like this have they seen, and what was the outcome?

Software doesn't have to be limited to the dozens of deals meeting specific criteria that a banker might see in a career; it has access to many thousands of data points that can be sorted and analyzed ad nauseam. Software will also be far less likely to have the kinds of biases that can afflict even the most self-aware of humans. In short, when you are making decisions based on experience, humans are not even close to being a match for software. It is impossible for us to replicate the lack of bias or the sheer volumes that computers were built to handle.

Does this mean you should leave banking to the machines? Absolutely not! If anything, the need to have top-notch lenders will become even more acute. An article in the *Harvard Business Review*, "The Simple Economics of Machine Intelligence[15]," explains why.

---

[15]   Agrawal, Ajay, Joshua Gans, and Avi Goldfarb. "The Simple Economics of Machine Intelligence." Harvard Business Review. N.p., 17 Nov. 2016. Web. 17 Feb. 2017. <https://hbr.org/2016/11/the-simple-economics-of-machine-intelligence>.

"The first effect of machine intelligence will be to lower the cost of goods and services that rely on prediction."

Translation: A bank's overhead lowers as it becomes cheaper to crunch the numbers and calculate the risks.

"When the cost of any input falls so precipitously, there are two other well-established economic implications. First, we will start using prediction to perform tasks where we previously didn't."

Translation: Banks will be able to look at deals from all sorts of different angles that were previously not possible. For example, with AI you'll be able to predict with much greater accuracy just how much a customer will use that line of credit they're applying for.

"Second, the value of other things that complement prediction will rise."

Translation: There are human nuances that machines don't understand, and all of those same meaningful transactions will still need a person to make the final decision. When the predictive powers become table stakes, the decision making of lenders will likely be the determining factor on many deals.

With AI, a person can make a far more informed decision. Well-designed software does much more than simply analyze reams of data; it actually boils that data down to useful and contextual insight that can be used to augment the human decision. It's why we often talk about AI as "augmented intelligence" or "amplified intelligence."

Banking Is a (Human) Relationship Business

AI is really just the next step in the improvement process for banks because at the end of the day, banking is still about humans connecting with each other. That connection isn't made on the golf course, by sending a holiday card, or during a power lunch. It's created through pricing, when a borrower sits down with a banker and they work together to create a deal that benefits both sides.

The relationships forged through those connections are the foundation upon which your bank's brand—and its future—rests. Put simply, they're what will enable your bank to "*Earn It*," now and in the years to come.